Thinking Through **Grammar**

A Prototype-Construction Course

Thinking Through **Grammar**

A Prototype-Construction Course

Arthur Whimbey
Myra J. Linden
Brad Frieswyk

BGF Performance Systems, LLC.
Chicago, IL

2004

BGF Performance Systems, LLC
Chicago, IL
1-800-481-3495
www.bgfperformance.com

ISBN 0-9709075-6-7

Cover design by Rojo Designs

Contents

CHAPTER

A BASIC SENTENCE: SUBJECT, ACTION VERB, OBJECT

Grammar is the study of how sentences are built. By studying grammar, you will learn to write more effective sentences. The exercises at the beginning of this book are very easy. But do not skip over them. Do them all. They form the basis for the advanced sentence patterns you will learn later in the text.

Here is a basic sentence:

> Cows eat grass.

This sentence has three parts. We will discuss these three parts because they play an important role in many sentences.

EXERCISE

Copy this sentence:

> Cows eat grass.

_____

The sentence you copied says that something performs an action on something else.

The word that names the action is called a <u>VERB</u>. Use this information to do the next exercise.

EXERCISE

Underline the verb in the sentence you copied above and write *verb* under it.

Here is the answer for the last exercise:

Cows <u>eat</u> grass.
     Verb

The word that names the thing that performs the action is called the <u>SUBJECT</u>. Use this information in the next exercise.

EXERCISE

Underline the subject in the sentence you copied and write the word *subject* under it.

Here is the answer for the last exercise:

<u>Cows</u> <u>eat</u> grass.
Subject *Verb*

The word that names the thing which receives the action is called the <u>OBJECT</u>.

EXERCISE

Underline the object in the sentence you copied and write the word *object* under it.

Here is the answer for the last exercise:

<u>Cows</u> <u>eat</u> <u>grass</u>.
Subject *Verb* *Object*

This answer shows the three major parts of the sentence: the subject, the verb, and the object. These three terms are used constantly in the study of grammar. Knowing what they refer to is extremely important.

Note About the Exercises:

In this book, the exercises are distributed throughout each chapter rather than being all placed at the end of the chapter. Furthermore, the exercises are placed in boxes to separate

them from the text. **The answer for an exercise is sometimes discussed right after the exercise. It is important that you do each exercise before reading the answer. You will gain the greatest benefit from the exercises if you try to answer them yourself before reading the explanation in the text.**

Here is a sentence similar to the one you worked on above:

Plumbers install sinks.

EXERCISES

1. Copy this sentence.

Plumbers install sinks.

_____

2. In the sentence you just copied, underline the word that names the action and write *verb* under it.

Here is the answer for Exercise 2:

Plumbers <u>*install*</u> *sinks.*
           Verb

Install is the verb. It names the action carried out by a plumber.

EXERCISE

Underline the subject in the sentence you just copied and write the word *subject* under it.

Here is the answer for the last exercise:

<u>*Plumbers*</u> <u>*install*</u> *sinks.*
  Subject   Verb

Plumbers is the subject of the sentence because plumbers carry out the activity named by the verb.

EXERCISE

In the sentence you just copied, underline the object and write the word *object* under it.

Here is the answer for the last exercise:

$$\underline{Plumbers} \quad \underline{install} \quad \underline{sinks}.$$
$$\text{Subject} \qquad \text{Verb} \qquad \text{Object}$$

Sinks names the object in the sentence because *sinks* receives the action.

Our analysis of the sentence shows that this sentence has the SUBJECT - VERB - OBJECT (SVO) pattern. As we analyze sentences, we will find this pattern again and again, even in very complicated sentences.

Almost all sentences found in books and magazines contain a subject and a verb, although some do not contain objects. They also contain other grammatical structures which make them richer and more complicated. We will study these other structures and put them all together as we progress through this book.

Understanding subjects and verbs is essential for understanding the rest of sentences. The next chapter looks at a basic relationship between subjects and verbs.

But first do the following exercises before turning to the next chapter.

EXERCISES

1. Copy this sentence.

   Automobiles consume gasoline.

   _____

2. Cross out the verb in the sentence you wrote and write *burn* above it.

3. Cross out the subject in the sentence you wrote and write *cars* above it.

4. Cross out the object in the sentence you wrote and write *fuel* above it.

Two words that have the same meaning are called "synonyms." *Cars* and *automobiles* are synonyms. In the last exercises you rewrote a sentence by replacing a word in each grammatical position with a synonym.

CHAPTER

2

SUBJECT-VERB AGREEMENT IN NUMBER

Compare these words.

> horse   horses

The word *horse* refers to just one horse. A word that refers to just one thing is called "singular."

EXERCISES

1. Write these two words.

   Singular   Plural

   _____   _____

2. Write *horse* under *Singular*.

3. Write *horses* under *Plural*.

The word *horses* refers to more than one horse. A word that refers to more than one thing is called "plural." Since both "horse" and "horses" can be used as the subject of a sentence, the subject of a sentence can be singular or plural.

Fill in the four empty spaces in this table.

Subject

Singular	Plural
horse	horses
cow	_____
automobile	_____
_____	cats
_____	nations

The table that you just completed shows that *s* is added to a singular subject to make it plural. But exactly the opposite is true of verbs. Adding an *s* to a verb makes it singular. It is made plural by dropping the *s* at the end.

Verb

Singular	Plural
eats	eat

You see the pattern in these sentences.

Singular Subject and Appropriate Verb

A horse eats grass.

Plural Subject and Appropriate Verb

Horses eat grass.

The first sentence has a singular subject. So the subject does not have an *s*, but the verb does have an *s*. The second sentence has a plural subject. So the subject has an *s*, but the verb does not have an *s*.

You can remember this pattern as the S/No-S Pattern.

If the subject has an *s*, the verb usually does not.

If the subject does not have an *s*, the verb usually does.

6

EXERCISES

1. Rewrite this sentence with *drinks* in the blank space.

   A cat _____ water.

   _____

2. Rewrite this sentence with *drink* in the blank space.

   Cats _____ water.

   _____

3. Rewrite this sentence with *chases* in the blank space.

   A dog _____ cats.

   _____

4. Rewrite this sentence with *chase* in the blank space.

   Dogs _____ cats.

   _____

The next exercise is a little different. You must decide which form of a verb belongs in a sentence.

EXERCISE

Rewrite the following sentences with *sell* in the blank space of one sentence and *sells* in the other.

   A. A butcher _____ meat.

   _____

   B. Butchers _____ meat.

   _____

In the last exercise, Sentence A has a singular subject (butcher), so it requires a verb with an *s*.

   A butcher *sells* meat.

7

Sentence B has a plural subject (butchers), so it requires a verb without an *s*.

Butchers *sell* meat.

Use the same reasoning for the following exercise.

EXERCISE

Rewrite the following sentence with *fight* in the blank space of one sentence and *fights* in the blank space of the other.

A. A firefighter _____ fires.

_____

B. Firefighters _____ fires.

_____

In the last exercise, Sentence A has a singular subject (firefighter), so it requires a verb with an *s*.

A firefighter *fights* fires.

Sentence B has a plural subject (firefighters), so it requires a verb without an *s*.

Firefighters *fight* fires.

EXERCISES

1. Rewrite the following sentences with *clean* in the blank space of one sentence and *cleans* in the other blank space.

A. A janitor _____ floors.

_____

B. Janitors _____ floors.

_____

2. Rewrite the following sentences with *protect* in one blank space and *protects* in the other.

   A. A soldier _____ a country.

   _____

   B. Soldiers _____ a country.

   _____

The next exercise is completely different. You must change both the subject and the verb in a sentence.

EXERCISE

Rewrite this sentence with a plural subject.

   A bee makes honey.

_____

In the last exercise, the first step is to add an *s* to the subject.

   bees

The next step is to drop the *s* from the verb.

   bees make

Sentences with singular subjects often begin with *a*. This *a* means "one." "A bee" means "one bee." Sentences with plural subjects never begin with *a*. We will omit the *a* from our answer. Here is the final answer.

   Bees make honey.

EXERCISE

Rewrite this sentence so that it has a plural subject.

   A fire destroys trees.

_____

9

In the last exercise, an *s* must be added to the subject and omitted from the verb.

Singular Subject: fire   destroy*s*   trees.

Plural Subject: fire*s*   destroy   trees

Here is the final answer.

Fires destroy trees.

EXERCISES

Rewrite each sentence so that it has a plural subject.

1. A squirrel collects nuts.

_____

2. A bird builds nests.

_____

3. A mathematician solves problems.

_____

4. A computer analyzes information.

_____

5. A lifeguard saves lives.

_____

6. A doughnut provides pleasure.

_____

The next group of exercises asks you to reverse the process. You will transform sentences with plural subjects into sentences with singular subjects.

EXERCISE

Rewrite this sentence so that it has a singular subject.

Barbers cut hair.

_____

In the last exercise, the first step is to delete the *s* from the subject.

barber

The next step is to add an *s* to the verb.

barber cuts

Then *hair* can be added.

barber cuts hair

Finally, *a* must be added in front. This *a* historically comes from the word *one*. Writing *a* in front ensures that the reader understands that the subject is singular. All of the answers for the remaining exercises in this chapter require an *a* in front.

Here is the answer for the last exercise.

A barber cuts hair.

EXERCISE

Rewrite this sentence so it has a singular subject.

Farmers grow food.

_____

The first step in answering the last exercise is to drop the *s* from the subject.

farmer

The next step is to add an *s* to the verb.

farmer grows

Finally, *a* is added at the beginning and *food* is added at the end.

A farmer grows food.

EXERCISES

Rewrite each sentence so it has a singular subject.

1. Bakers bake cakes.

_____

2. Toasters toast bread.

_____

3. Comedians amuse people.

_____

4. Stores sell merchandise.

_____

5. Politicians deliver speeches.

_____

Making sure that singular verbs are matched with singular subjects and plural verbs with plural subjects is called checking for subject-verb agreement in number. This is easy to do for simple sentences, such as those in the above exercises. But it is not always so easy to do for complicated sentences with a dozen or more words placed between the subject and the verb. However, now that you understand the pattern underlying subject-verb agreement, you will have no difficulty with the more complicated sentences. We will discuss and practice subject-verb agreement again with complicated sentences later in the book.

Exceptions to the *s*/no-*s* pattern: The *s*/no-*s* memory aid occasionally does not work. Some words used as subjects of sentences are made plural by changing their spelling rather than by adding an *s*. Here are three examples.

__Singular__	__Plural__
woman	women
child	children
mouse	mice

Also, some singular subjects end with an *s*, such as *glass* in the sentence, "Glass breaks easily."

But the pattern of matching a singular subject with a singular verb and a plural subject with a plural verb still applies:

A mouse *eats* cheese.
Mice *eat* cheese.

Because the subject of the second sentence (*Mice*) is plural, the verb does not have an *s*.

CREATING PAST TENSE VERBS

To turn a statement about the present into a sentence about the past, usually *ed* is added to the verb. However, there are some complications with the past tense which we will discuss shortly.

EXERCISES

1. Copy this sentence.

   My brothers open the store every morning.

   _____

2. Underline the verb in the sentence and write *verb* under it.

3. Underline the subject in the sentence and write *subject* under it.

4. Underline the object in the sentence and write *object* under it

---

Here is the answer for Exercises 2-4.

   My <u>brothers</u> <u>open</u> the <u>store</u> every morning.
       Subject   Verb   Object

This answer shows the three main parts of the original sentence. The words *every morning* at the end of the entire sentence are not part of the object. They give additional information. From now on, many of the sentences you deal with will have additional information. The grammatical role of such additional information will be discussed in later chapters.

EXERCISE

Rewrite this sentence with *ed* added to the verb.

My brothers open the store every morning.

_____

Here is the answer for the last exercise:

My brothers **opened** the store every morning.

This sentence shows how to make a statement about the past. Adding *ed* to the verb changes a statement about the present into a statement about the past.

EXERCISES

Rewrite these sentences so they make statements about the past by adding *ed* to their verbs.

1. Our cats knock the ornaments off our Christmas tree.

_____

2. Our dogs smell the roast beef in your shopping bag.

_____

If the verb in a sentences ends with *e*, just add *d* not *ed* to make a statement about the past.

EXERCISE

Rewrite this sentence so that it makes a statement about the past by adding *d* to the verb.

The umpires ignore the rude comments of some fans.

_____

In the last exercise, the first step is to find the verb. Here is a grammatical analysis of the three main parts of the sentence.

The <u>umpires</u> <u>ignore</u> the <u>rude comments</u>
     Subject   Verb   Object

Since the verb ends in *e*, only a *d* needs to be added.

The umpires ***ignored*** the rude comments of some fans.

EXERCISE

Rewrite the sentence so that it makes a statement about the past by adding *d* to the verb.

My cousins praise the beauty of Germany's mountains and forests.

_____

If the verb in a sentence ends with an *s* used to create a singular verb, the *s* must be dropped before adding *ed* or *d*.

EXERCISE

Rewrite this sentence with *s* dropped from the verb and *ed* added to the verb.

My cousin delivers newspapers before breakfast.

_____

In the last exercise, the verb in the sentence is *delivers*. To make this a past tense verb, the *s* must be deleted and *ed* must be added.

This is the final answer:

My cousin ***delivered*** newspapers before breakfast.

EXERCISE

Rewrite this sentence so it refers to the past by dropping *s* from the verb and adding *ed* to it.

My uncle waters his lawn in the morning.

_____

In grammar the word "tense" generally refers to time. A **present tense** verb is used to discuss a current activity. A **past tense** verb is used to discuss an action that happened in the past.

EXERCISES

1. Copy this sentence and underline the verb.

   Dad worked at the Ford factory.

   _____

2. For the sentence you just copied, write *present tense* under the verb if it is a present tense verb. But write *past tense* if it is a past tense verb.

3. Copy this sentence and underline the verb.

   Lester works in the Del Monte factory.

   _____

4. For the sentence you just copied, write *present tense* under the verb if it is a present tense verb. But write *past tense* if it is a past tense verb.

This chapter provides an introduction to writing sentences about the past. The next chapter discusses a complication that can arise in writing such sentences.

CHAPTER

IRREGULAR VERBS

Some verbs are not made past tense by adding *ed* or *d* at the end. Instead the past tense form of the verb differs from the basic form in some other way. For example, the past tense of *tell* is *told*. Use this fact for the next exercise.

EXERCISE

Rewrite this sentence to indicate that the action took place in the past.

Dad tells ghost stories to the children on Halloween.

_____

The last exercise asks you to rewrite the sentence to indicate that the action occurred in the past. This means that the present tense verb must be replaced by its past tense form. *Tell* must be replaced by *told*.

Dad ***told*** ghost stories to the children on Halloween.

Verbs such as *tell* are called **irregular** because we do not construct their past tense form in the "regular" way. Instead, we learn their past tense form through exposure to the language — through reading widely and listening to the speech of educated people. Here are six common irregular verbs and their past tense forms.

Present Tense	**Past Tense**
think	thought
write	wrote
sing	sang
make	made
give	gave
sell	sold

EXERCISES

1. If *think* was a regular verb, what would its past tense form be? _____

2. According to the table above, what is the actual past tense form of *think*? _____

If *think* was a regular verb, its past tense form would be constructed by adding *ed* at the end. So the past tense form would be *thinked*.

EXERCISE

If *write* was a regular verb, what would its past tense form be? _____

Since *write* ends with an *e*, only *d* would be added to construct its past tense form. Thus, its past tense form would be *writed*.

EXERCISES

1. What are verbs called if their past tense forms are not constructed in the "regular" way?

   _____

2. Rewrite each of the following sentences to indicate that the action took place in the past.

   a. Sarah sings at weddings.

   _____

   b. Composers write songs for special occasions.

   _____

   c. Stores sell a lot of merchandise right before the holidays.

   _____

   d. Musicians give concerts for charitable purposes.

   _____

CHAPTER

INTRANSITIVE VERBS

In the sentences we have studied so far, the verb is followed by an object.

Lassie <u>eats</u>   <u>spaghetti</u>.
            Verb   Object

The object is the thing that receives the action named by the verb. But some sentences do not include an object. Here is an example.

Lassie eats quickly.

Quickly is not an object. It is not the thing that receives the action. It describes the action. Words like *quickly* are discussed later in the book.

EXERCISES

1. Copy this sentence.

John broke a glass.

_____

2. Underline the subject in the sentence you just copied and write *subject* under it.

3. Underline the verb in the sentence you just copied and write *verb* under it.

---

4. Underline the object in the sentence you copied and write *object* under it.

5. Copy this sentence.

   The glass broke.

   _____

6. Underline the subject in the sentence you just copied and write *subject* under it.

7. Underline the verb in this sentence and write *verb* under it.

8. Does the sentence contain an object?

   Write YES or NO _____

For some purposes, it is useful to know whether the verb in a sentence has an object. Therefore, a special term has been developed. A verb that has an object is called "transitive."

EXERCISE

One of the following sentences contains an object, the other does not.

   Marsha writes novels.
   Marsha writes well.

Copy the sentence that has an object.

_____

Underline the object and write *object* beneath it.

In the last exercise, *novels* is the object of *writes*. A novel receives the writer's action. But *well* is not an object. *Well* describes the writing.

   Marsha writes novels.
     S   V   O

   Marsha writes well.
     S   V   Evaluation

A verb that does not have an object is called "**intransitive**."

A verb that does have an object is called "**transitive**."

EXERCISES

1. Copy these sentences and underline the verb in each one.

    A. Jim threw the football.

_____

    B. Jim threw accurately.

_____

2. Write *transitive* under the verb that does have an object.

3. Write *intransitive* under the verb that does not have an object.

In the last set of exercises, the verb (*threw*) is followed by an object (*football*) in Sentence A. Therefore, *threw* is a transitive verb in Sentence A. The word "transitive" is related to "transport" and "transfer." A transitive verb "transfers" the action from the subject to the object. "Intransitive" means "not transitive." An intransitive verb does not "transport" the action from the subject to an object. It just describes the action of the subject.

Even though intransitive verbs do not have objects, they are considered verbs because they behave like verbs in other ways. For example, adding *ed* shows that the action happened in the past.

EXERCISE

Rewrite this sentence to indicate that the action occurred in the past.

    Our baby crawls proudly.

_____

In the last exercise, the verb in the sentence is intransitive because it lacks an object. Yet it is made past tense by deleting the *s* ending from the verb and adding *ed*.

    Our baby *crawled* proudly.

EXERCISE

Rewrite this sentence to show that the action occurred in the past.

My truck starts noisely.

_____

Many students hear the term "intransitive" verb in their English classes. But they never learn exactly what it means, and they remain a little intimidated by it for their entire school years. You now know what this term means. An intransitive verb is simply a verb without an object in a sentence.

STATIVE VERBS: VERBS EXPRESSING MENTAL STATES AND VARIOUS RELATIONSIPS

Some verbs do not represent actions. Such a verb is illustrated in the next exercises.

EXERCISES

1. Copy this sentence below.

    That suitcase contains your diamond ring.

    _____

2. Underline the subject and write *subject* under it.

3. Underline the verb and write *verb* under it.

4. Underline the object and write *object* under it.

The verb *contains* does not represent an action. It says that one thing is inside another thing, so it represents a spatial relationship. It tells the location of something.

But grammatically, *contains* is the verb in the sentence because it plays the role of a verb. It connects the subject with the object, and it changes form to show whether a situation was true in the past or is true in the present. This is shown in the next exercise.

EXERCISE

Rewrite the sentence so that it says the situation was true in the past.

That suitcase contains your diamond ring.

_____

To say that the situation was true in the past, the past tense form of the verb *contain* is needed. Therefore, *ed* must be added to *contain*.

That suitcase contained your diamond ring.

A verb like *contain* that does not express an action is called a "stative" verb. Another stative verb is *own*. The next exercise shows that it changes just like an action verb to indicate whether the subject is singular or plural.

EXERCISE

Rewrite this sentence with the subject made plural.

A king owns everything in a country.

_____

To make the subject plural, *a king* must be changed to *kings*. But the verb must also be made plural: *owns* must be changed to *own*.

Kings own everything in a country.

Several more stative verbs are illustrated in the next exercises.

The sentence in the last exercise contains a past tense verb. To make the verb present tense, *d* must be omitted. Also, because the subject is singular, an *s* must be added to the verb.

My cat despises my dog.

Note that *despises* is a mental state. Many mental states are represented by stative verbs, including *love*, *hate*, and *admire*.

EXERCISE

1. Rewrite this sentence to indicate that the situation it describes is true at the present time.

Lazy George's attitude angered his hard-working father.

_____

2. Rewrite this sentence to indicate that the situation it describes was true in the past.

Sue's cooperation pleases her supervisor at work.

_____

3. Rewrite this sentence with the subject changed from singular to plural.

A skeleton frightens the toddlers at the Halloween party.

_____

CHAPTER

USING *WILL* TO WRITE ABOUT THE FUTURE

Here is a sentence about a present situation.

Roy plays football for our team.

To change this to a sentence about the future, the word *will* must be added before the verb.

EXERCISE

Rewrite this sentence with *will* inserted before *plays* and with *plays* changed to *play*.

Roy plays football for our team.

_____

In the last exercise, when *will* was added before the verb *plays*, the *s* had to be dropped from *plays*. In general, when *will* is placed before a verb, the base form of the verb is used.

The base form of a verb is the form without an extra *s* or *ed* at the end. A verb like *play* has several forms. Three of the forms are shown in the following table.

Some Forms of a Verb
Base Form   s Form   ed Form
play   plays   played

The *ed* form is used to talk about the past. The *s* form is used in talking about the present when the subject of a sentence is singular. The base form is considered the primary form. It is the form of the verb you will find in the dictionary. Sentences about the future always use the base form of the verb. This fact is illustrated by the following exercise:

EXERCISE

Rewrite this sentence with *will* inserted before *drives* and with *drives* changed to *drive*.

Ivan drives a taxi for extra money.

_____

The next exercise presents a sentence about the past. You are asked to rewrite it so it concerns the future.

EXERCISE

Rewrite this sentence with *will* inserted before *stayed* and *stayed* changed to *stay*.

Irene stayed late to complete her painting.

_____

In the last exercise, the verb *stayed* is a past tense verb. It is used to make a statement about the past. When *will* is placed before it to make a statement about the future, its base form (*stay*) must be used.

EXERCISE

Rewrite this sentence with *will* inserted before *sings* and *sings* changed to *sing*.

Kathy sings with my brother's band.

_____

When *will* is placed before a verb, *will* is called a "helping" verb. It helps the main verb by allowing it to talk about the future.

A pair of words like *will sing* is called a "verb phrase."

Kathy *will sing* with my brother's band.
Verb Phrase

A "phrase" is two or more words used together to play some role in a sentence. In a "verb phrase," the main word is a verb.

EXERCISES

1. Rewrite the following sentence with *helping* in the blank space.

   When *will* is placed before a verb, *will* is called a ____ verb.

   _____

2. Rewrite this sentence with *phrase* in the blank space.

   A ____ is two or more words used together to play some role in a sentence.

   _____

3. Rewrite the following sentence with *verb phrase* in the blank space.

   A pair of words like *will sing*, which consists of a helping verb and a main verb, is called a ____.

   _____

4. Rewrite this sentence so it makes a statement about the future rather than the past by changing *received* to *will receive*.

   Pamela received a new bicycle for her birthday.

   _____

5. Rewrite this sentence so that it makes a statement about the future rather than the past by changing *ate* to *will eat*.

   We ate dinner at one of the nicest restaurants in Chicago.

   _____

6. Rewrite this sentence so that it makes a statement about the future by inserting *will* before *enjoys* and changing *enjoys* to *enjoy*.

Angela enjoys playing volley ball for our team.

_____

CHAPTER

8

SPECIAL PEOPLE (*YOU* AND *I*) REQUIRE SPECIAL VERB PATTERNS

You and I are special people. So a special verb pattern is used when *you* or *I* is the subject of a sentence. The pattern is illustrated in the following exercise.

EXERCISE

Rewrite this sentence with *Suzie* replaced by *you* and *writes* replaced by *write.*

Suzie writes well.

____

The next exercise also illustrates the pattern.

EXERCISE

Rewrite this sentence with *Jane* replaced by *you* and *walks* replaced by *walk*.

Jane walks quickly.

_____

The answers for the last two exercises show that when *you* is the subject of a sentence, the base form of the verb rather than the *s* form is the correct present tense form of the verb. The same pattern is used when the subject is *I*, as shown in the next exercise.

EXERCISE

Rewrite this sentence with *Frank* replaced by *I* and *eats* replaced by *eat*.

Frank eats too much candy.

_____

The answers for the last three exercises illustrate the following rule.

> **When the subject of a sentence is *you* or *I*, the base form of the verb is the correct present tense form. The base form of the verb is the form without an *s*.**

Use the above rule in the next exercises.

EXERCISE

Rewrite this sentence with *Dennis* replaced by *you* and the appropriate form of the verb.

Dennis drinks too much sugar-filled soda.

_____

In the last exercise, when the subject is changed from *Dennis* to *you*, the verb must be changed to the base form *drink*.

You *drink* too much sugar-filled soda.

The subjects *you* and *I* do not use a special pattern with past tense verbs. The same past tense verbs are used with *you* and *I* as with all other subjects. This fact is illustrated by the following exercise.

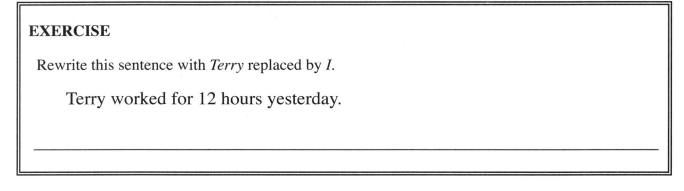

EXERCISE

Rewrite this sentence with *Terry* replaced by *I*.

Terry worked for 12 hours yesterday.

_____

Here is the original sentence from the last exercise and answer.

Terry *worked* for 12 hours yesterday.

I *worked* for 12 hours yesterday.

We know that both sentences concern past situations because they both use the past tense verb *worked*. Comparing the sentences shows that the same past tense verb is used for the subject *I* as for other subjects, such as *Terry*.

Just as sentences about the past do not use a special verb pattern for *you* and *I*, sentences about the future also do not use a special pattern. This fact is illustrated in the next exercises.

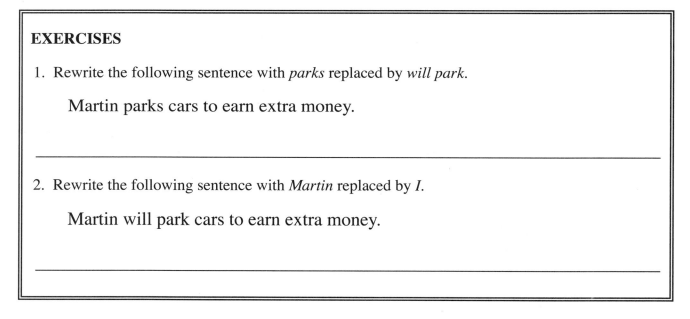

EXERCISES

1. Rewrite the following sentence with *parks* replaced by *will park*.

   Martin parks cars to earn extra money.

   _____

2. Rewrite the following sentence with *Martin* replaced by *I*.

   Martin will park cars to earn extra money.

   _____

Exercise 1 above shows how to change a sentence about the present into a sentence about the future with a typical subject like *Martin*. Exercise 2 shows that the same verb phrase (*will park*) is used when the subject is *I*. A special verb pattern is not used to write future tense sentences when *you* or *I* is the subject.

In summary, a special verb pattern is used with *you* and *I* only for present tense sentences. The following exercises provide additional illustrations of that special verb pattern, which can be stated as follows: When the subject of a sentence is *you* or *I*, the base form of a verb is the correct present tense form.

EXERCISES

1. Rewrite this sentence with *Larry* replaced by *you* and *plays* replaced by *play*.

   Larry plays video games for too many hours a day.

   _____

2. Rewrite this sentence with *John* replaced by *you* and with *talks* replaced by *talk*.

   John talks too much during math class.

   _____

3. Rewrite this sentence with *Marcia* replaced by *I* and *plans* replaced by *plan*.

   Marcia plans to attend law school after graduating from college.

   _____

4. Rewrite this sentence with *George* replaced by *I* and with *likes* replaced by *like*.

   George likes to visit the zoo and watch the animals, especially the monkeys.

   _____

CHAPTER

A SPECIAL FAMILY OF VERBS: *IS, WAS, ARE,* AND *WERE*

This chapter concerns a special type of sentence and a special family of verbs. The sentences we have worked with so far have described the activities of subjects, as well as the relationships between subjects and objects.

But now we will consider sentences that describe the subjects themselves. The difference is illustrated in the next exercises.

EXERCISES

Compare these sentences. One describes Bob. The other describes an action performed by Bob.

    Sentence A: Bob is tall.

    Sentence B: Bob repairs cars.

1. Write the sentence describing an action performed by Bob.

_____

---

2. Write the sentence that describes Bob.

_____

Sentence A is about Bob himself. Sentence B is about an action performed by Bob. This chapter discusses sentences like Sentence A.

EXERCISES

1. Rewrite this sentence with *is* in the blank space.

    Ted _____ underweight.

    _____

2. Rewrite this sentence with *is* in the blank space.

    Paul _____ a lifeguard.

    _____

In the two sentences you just wrote, *is* is the verb.

The verb *is* is a special verb that is often used in sentences describing the subject. The verb *is* is different from other verbs in several ways.

For one thing, its plural form is not formed the way that the plural forms of other verbs are. The following exercise shows how the plural forms of action verbs are formed.

EXERCISE

Rewrite this sentence with *a cat* replaced by *cats* and with the *s* omitted from the verb.

    A cat climbs trees.

    _____

Here is the answer for the last exercise.

Cats climb trees.

The plural form of the verb is formed by omitting the *s*.

Singular	**Plural**
climbs	climb

But the plural form of *is* is not formed by just omitting the *s*. Instead a totally different word is used. **The plural form of *is* is *are*.**

Singular	**Plural**
is	are

EXERCISES

1. Rewrite this sentence with *a dog* replaced by *dogs* and *is* replaced by *are*.

    A dog is intelligent.

    _____

2. Rewrite this sentence with *a teacher* replaced by *teachers* and *is* replaced by its plural form.

    A teacher is happy when students learn.

    _____

In the last exercise, the verb *is* must be replaced by its plural form, which is *are*. Here is the answer.

Teachers *are* happy when students learn.

EXERCISES

1. Rewrite this sentence with *the horse* replaced by *horses* and *is* replaced by its plural form.

    The horse is no longer an important source of power for farming and transportation.

    _____

---

2. Rewrite this sentence with *roosters* replaced by *a rooster* and *are* replaced by *is*.

> Roosters are noisy in the morning.

_____

3. Rewrite this sentence with *automobiles* replaced by *an automobile* and *are* replaced by *is*.

> Automobiles are more than just a form of transportation for most people.

_____

4. Rewrite this sentence with *a computer* replaced by *computers* and with *is* replaced by its plural form.

> A computer is very useful for a person who types long papers and books.

_____

5. Rewrite this sentence with *a democratic government* replaced by *democratic governments* and *is* replaced by *are*.

> A democratic government is controlled by the governed.

_____

The verb *is* differs from other verbs not only in the way it is made plural but also in the way its past tense is formed. The past tense is not formed by adding *ed*.

Instead a completely different word is used for the past tense:

The past tense of *is* is *was*.

EXERCISES

In each exercise, rewrite the sentence so that it describes a situation which existed in the past by replacing *is* with *was*.

> 1. John Wayne is a great actor.

_____

39

2. Texas is the largest state in the United States.

_____

3. Massachusetts is an English colony.

_____

4. Cynthia is the tallest girl on our basketball team.

_____

The verb *is* has still another form. **The past tense form of *is* for plural subjects is *were*.** All other verbs have just one past tense form. But *is* has two past tense forms. One is used for singular subjects. The other is used for plural subjects. These facts are illustrated by the following exercises.

EXERCISE

1. Rewrite this sentence with *is* in the blank space.

Dave _____ late.

_____

2. Rewrite this sentence with *was* in the blank space.

Dave _____ late for class yesterday.

_____

3. Rewrite this sentence with *were* in the blank space.

Dave and Ed _____ late for class yesterday.

_____

The answer for Exercise 2 shows that *was* is the past tense form of *is* used with singular subjects. The answer for Exercise 3 shows that *were* is the past tense form of *is* used with plural subjects.

EXERCISES

1. Rewrite this sentence with *a student* replaced by *two students* and *is* replaced by *were*.

   A student is waiting to see the principal.

   _____

2. Rewrite this sentence so it describes a past situation by replacing *are* with *were*.

   Horses are used to pull plows and wagons.

   _____

3. Rewrite this sentence so it describes a past situation by replacing *are* with *were*.

   Automobiles are the major source of air pollution.

   _____

Here are several more exercises that illustrate the use of *is, are, was,* and *were.*

EXERCISES

1. Singular Subject, Present Tense: *is*. Rewrite this sentence with *is* in the blank.

   A cat _____ sitting on your car.

   _____

2. Plural Subject, Present Tense: *are*. Rewrite this sentence with *are* in the blank.

   Two cats _____ are sitting on your car.

   _____

3. Singular Subject, Past Tense: *was*. Rewrite this sentence with *was* in the blank.

   A cat _____ sitting on your car last night.

   _____

41

4. Plural Subject, Past Tense: *were*. Rewrite this sentence with *were* in the blank.

Two cats _____ sitting on your car last night.

_____

5. Make a table like this:

	Singular	Plural
Present		
Past		

6. Write either *is, are, was,* or *were* in each box of your table.

Summary: This chapter presented four forms of a special verb: *is, are, was,* and *were*. The following exercises provide additional illustrations of their usage.

EXERCISES

1. Rewrite this sentence so it describes a past situation by replacing *is* with *was*.

A bullfrog is sitting on a lily pad in the pond.

_____

2. Rewrite this sentence so it describes a present situation by replacing *was* with *is*.

Bessie was very wet from the storm.

_____

3. Rewrite this sentence so it describes a past situation by replacing *are* with *were*.

Three first-graders are lost in Disney World.

_____

4. Rewrite this sentence so it describes a present situation by replacing *were* with *are*.

Several computers were needed to solve all this company's information processing problems.

_____

The family of verbs that includes *is, are, was,* and *were* will be described in more detail in the next five chapters.

CHAPTER

WRITING ABOUT THE FUTURE:
THE BASE FORM BE

Chapter 7 explains that to make a statement about the future, *will* is written before the base form of the verb in a sentence. But the verb *is* has so many forms (*is, are, was, were*), that determining its base form can be puzzling. What is its base form? The base form of this verb is shown in the next exercise.

EXERCISE

Rewrite this sentence so it makes a statement about the future by replacing *is* with *will be*.

Don is sorry.

_____

Here is the answer for the last exercise.

Don *will be* sorry.

This answer shows that the base form for the family of verbs that includes *is, are, was,* and *were* is *be*.

The English language developed over hundreds of years and adopted words from many different languages. Grammarians have studied the history of English and have explained how *is, are, was, were,* and *be* all came to be part of the same verb family. We do not have time to review the history of that verb family here. We can simply show how the different forms are used today in Standard Written English.

EXERCISES

1. Rewrite this sentence with *is* replaced by *will be.*

   A car is driven by an accident-free computer rather than its human owner.

   _____

2. Rewrite this sentence so that it makes a statement about the future by replacing *are* with *will be.*

   Computers are owned by most young children.

   _____

3. Is the subject in your answer for the last exercise singular or plural? Write your answer.

   _____

Your answers for the last exercises show that *will be* is used with plural subjects as well as singular subjects. The next exercises confirm that *be* is in the same verb family as *was* and *were.*

EXERCISES

1. Rewrite this sentence with *was* replaced by *will be.*

   A dog was on the spaceship.

   _____

2. Rewrite this sentence with *were* replaced by *will be.*

   Two chimpanzees were on the spaceship.

   _____

The verb *be* can never be used alone as a main verb. For example, *be* is used incorrectly in this sentence.

Leo be my best friend.

The error is corrected in the next exercise.

EXERCISE

Rewrite this sentence with *be* replaced by *is*.

Leo be my best friend.

_____

The next two exercises illustrate two more erroneous uses of *be* as a main verb.

EXERCISES

In each exercise, rewrite the sentence with *be* replaced by *are*.

1. Oranges be full of vitamin C.

_____

2. The Yankees and Cubs be the teams to watch.

_____

The remaining exercises show additional examples of changing *is, are, was,* or *were* to *will be* in order to make a statement about the future.

EXERCISES

1. Rewrite this sentence with *is* replaced by *will be*.

Reasonably priced housing is difficult to locate.

_____

2. Rewrite this sentence with *are* replaced by *will be*.

Clean rivers are hard to find.

_____

---

3. Rewrite this sentence with *was* replaced by *will be*.

Our team's quarterback was better than any other quarterback in the league.

_____

4. Rewrite this sentence with *were* replaced by *will be*.

The Christmas presents were hidden in the closet.

_____

CHAPTER

11

THE PRESENT PROGRESSIVE TENSE
WITH A SINGULAR SUBJECT

So far we have discussed the uses of *is, are, was,* and *were* as main verbs. They can also be used as helping verbs, as illustrated in the following exercise.

EXERCISE

Rewrite this sentence with *is* inserted before *repairs* and with *repairs* replaced by *repairing*.

Frank repairs our car.

In answering the last exercise, the first step is to insert *is* before *repairs*.

Frank *is* repairs

The next step is to replace *repairs* with *repairing*.

Frank is *repairing*

Here is the final answer.

> Frank is repairing our car.

EXERCISES

Compare these sentences.

> Sentence A: Frank repairs our car.
> Sentence B: Frank is repairing our car.

1. Write the sentence that says Frank is working on our car right now, at this minute.

   _____

2. Write the sentence that says Frank repairs our car when it needs to be repaired, but he may not be working on it right now.

Sentence A says that Frank repairs our car when it needs to be repaired. It does not say he is working on it right now.

Sentence B says Frank is working on the car right now, at the present moment.

The verb *repair* is called a present tense verb, but this is a little misleading. Such a verb is generally used in a sentence that describes an action which occurs regularly (often) but may not be occurring right now.

To indicate that an action is occurring at the present moment, a verb phrase like *is repairing* is generally used.

EXERCISE

Rewrite this sentence with *is* inserted before *eats* and with *ing* added to the base form of *eats*.

> Helen eats clams.

   _____

To answer the last exercise, *is* must be inserted before *eats*.

> Helen *is* eats

Then *ing* must be added to the base form of *eats*.

Recall that the base form of a verb is the form without an *s*.

Base Form   **s Form**

eat   eats

The instructions say to add *ing* to the base form.

eat + ing = eating

Here is the final answer.

Helen is eating clams.

EXERCISES

Compare these sentences.

Sentence A: Helen eats clams.
Sentence B: Helen is eating clams.

1. Write the sentence that says Helen is eating clams right now.

_____

2. Write the sentence which says that clams are eaten by Helen, although she might not be eating them right now.

_____

Not everybody likes clams. Some people never eat clams. Sentence A says that Helen does eat clams. But it does not say she is eating them right now.

To say that Helen is eating clams right now, Sentence B is used. Its verb phrase (*is eating*) indicates that Helen is eating clams right now.

A verb phrase like *is eating* is called a "progressive" verb phrase. The word "progressive" is related to the word "progress." An action that is "in progress" is occurring at the present time. Therefore a progressive verb phrase describes an action that is occurring at the present time.

EXERCISE

Rewrite this sentence with *is* inserted before *plays* and with *ing* added to the base form of *plays*.

Larry plays hockey.

_____

In answering the last exerecise, the first step is to insert *is* before *plays*.

Larry *is* plays

Then *ing* must be added to the base form of *plays*. The base form of *plays* is *play*.

Larry is *playing*

Here is the final answer.

Larry is playing hockey.

EXERCISES

Compare these sentences.

Sentence A: Larry plays hockey.
Sentence B: Larry is playing hockey.

1. Write the sentence that says Larry is playing hockey right now.

_____

2. Rewrite the following sentence with *progressive* in the blank space.

A verb phrase like "is playing" is called ____ because it describes an action "in progress."

_____

EXERCISES

Each of the following exercises presents a sentence that says a person engages in some activity regularly. You will write the sentence to say that the person is performing the activity right now.

1. Rewrite this sentence with *is* inserted before *drives* and with *drives* changed to *driving*.

Dad drives Billy to school.

_____

2. Rewrite this sentence with *is* inserted before *works* and with *ing* added to the base form of *works*.

    Carlos works at Disney World.

    _____

3. Rewrite this sentence with *is* inserted before *feeds* and with *ing* added to the base form of *feeds*.

    Lisa feeds our cats, who are quite fussy about what they eat.

    _____

4. Rewrite this sentence with the present tense verb *cuts* replaced by its progressive form.

    Dan cuts Linda's hair quite short.

    _____

12

THE PRESENT PROGRESSIVE TENSE WITH A PLURAL SUBJECT

Here is an exercise from the last chapater. Please write the answer again:

EXERCISE

Rewrite this sentence with a progressive verb.

Larry plays hockey.

_____

Note that the verb (*plays*) in the above exercise is singular and present tense.

Larry *plays* hockey
        Singular
     Present Tense

The answer uses the helping verb *is* because it is the singular, present tense member of the family *is*, *are*, *was*, and *were*.

Larry is playing hockey.

All the exercises in the last chapter include singular subjects and present tense verbs. Therefore they all use *is* to form the progressive tense.

In this chapter, all the exercises have plural subjects and present tense verbs. Therefore they all use the helping verb *are* to form the progressive tense.

	Singular	Plural
Present	is	**ARE**
Past	was	were

EXERCISE

Rewrite this sentence with *are* inserted before *swim* and with *swim* replaced by *swimming*.

My children swim in my neighbor's pool.

_____

In the last exercise, the subject of the sentence *children* is plural. Therefore the plural helping verb *are* is required for the progressive verb phrase *are swimming*.

My children *are swimming* in my neighbor's pool.
      Progressive
      Verb Phrase

This sentence says that the children are right now swimming in the neighbor's pool. The original sentence in this exercise does not say this. It only says that the children sometimes swim in the neighbor's pool.

EXERCISE

Rewrite this sentence with *are* inserted before *twinkle* and *twinkle* replaced by its *ing* form.

The lights twinkle down in the city.

_____

When *ing* is added to *twinkle*, the *e* is dropped.

twinkle → twinkl → twinkl*ing*

Here is the answer.

The lights are twinkling down in the city.

EXERCISES

1. Rewrite this sentence so it describes an activity occurring now by inserting *are* before *bark* and adding *ing* to *bark*.

   Our dogs bark at the garbageman.

   _____

2. Rewrite this sentence so it describes an activity occurring right now by inserting *are* before *play* and adding *ing* to *play*.

   Our children play in the school yard.

   _____

This chapter has discussed present progressive verb phrases in sentences with plural subjects. Such verb phrases are called "plural present progressive verb phrases." The next chapter discusses past tense progressive verb phrases. Which verbs from the *is, are, was, were* family do you think will be used as helping verbs?

CHAPTER

13

THE PAST PROGRESSIVE TENSE

Just as an activity can be occurring (in progress) at the present time, it could have been in progress at some time in the past. The answer for the following exercise describes such an activity.

EXERCISE

Rewrite this sentence with *was* inserted before *watched* and with *ing* added to the base form of *watched*.

Jim watched his regular TV when the electricity went off.

_____

In answering the last exercise, the first step is to write *was* before *watched*.

Jim *was* watched

Next *ing* must be added to the base form of *watched*. The base form of *watched* is *watch*.

<u>**Base Form**</u>	<u>***ed* Form**</u>
watch	watched

watch + ing = watching

Here is the final answer.

Jim was watching his regular TV when the electricity went off.

EXERCISE

Compare these sentences.

Sentence A: Jim watched his regular TV when the electricity went off.

Sentence B: Jim was watching his regular TV when the electricity went off.

1. Write the sentence which says Jim did the impossible: He watched TV when the electricity went off.

_____

2. Write the sentence which says that at the time the electricity went off, Jim was watching TV.

_____

A verb phrase like *was watching* is called a "past progressive" verb phrase because it is used in describing an action that was in progress in the past. Sentence B uses the past progressive verb phrase *was watching* to say that Jim was actually watching TV when the electricity went off.

The next exercise presents a sentence whose meaning is not clear until its past tense verb is replaced by a past progressive phrase.

EXERCISE

Rewrite this sentence with *was* inserted before *took* and with *took* replaced by its *ing* form.

Rick took a shower when the water to his entire apartment house was turned off.

_____

In answering the last exercise, the first step is to insert *was* before *took*.

Rick *was* took

Next, we need the *ing* form of *took*. *Took* is the past tense form of the verb *take*.

Base Form	**Past Tense Form**
take	took

Usually the past tense form is the *ed* form. But *take* is an irregular verb whose past tense form is *took*. The *ing* form of *take* is *taking*.

Here is the final answer.

> Rick was taking a shower when the water to his entire apartment house was turned off.

EXERCISES

Compare these sentences.

> Sentence A: Rick took a shower when the water to his entire apartment house was turned off.

> Sentence B: Rick was taking a shower when the water to his entire apartment house was turned off.

1. Write the sentence that contains a past progressive verb phrase. Then underline this verb phrase and write *past progressive* under it.

_____

2. Write the sentence that says Rick did the seemingly impossible: He took a shower without water.

_____

Sentence A might be included as an attention-getter in an advertisement for a new product that allows a person to shower without regular water. Otherwise, it does not seem to make much sense. The past progressive verb phrase *was taking* is needed to describe what probably did occur.

The past progressive verb phrase *was taking* uses the helping verb *was*. *Was* is a singular past tense verb. A singular helping verb is used in the last exercise because the subject of the sentence (*Rick*) is singular.

In the next exercise, a plural helping verb is used.

```
EXERCISE

Rewrite this sentence with were inserted before chased and with the verb chased changed to its
ing form.

    Our dogs chased our cats when we got home.

_____
```

In answering the last exercise, the first step is inserting *were* before *chased*.

> Our dogs *were* chased

Next, the *ing* form of *chased* is needed. It is shown in the following table.

Base Form	***ed* Form**	***ing* Form**
chase	chased	chasing

The *ing* form of *chase* must replace *chased*.

> Our dogs were *chasing*

Here is the final answer.

> Our dogs were chasing our cats when we got home.

In the last sentence, the plural verb *were* is used as a helping verb because the subject (*dogs*) is plural. *Were* is also used in the next exercise.

```
EXERCISE

Rewrite this sentence with were inserted before attempted and with attempted replaced by its ing
form.

    A few cars attempted to get somewhere on the icy streets, but most drivers
    stayed home.

_____
```

Be Never a Helping Verb in Progressive Verb Phrases

In standard written English, the verb *be* is never used as a helping verb in a progressive verb phrase. For example, the following sentence contains an error.

The kittens be drinking the milk out of Dad's cereal bowl.

You will correct the error in the next exercise.

EXERCISE

Rewrite this sentence with *be* replaced by *are*.

The kittens be drinking the milk out of Dad's cereal bowl.

_____

The helping verb in a progressive verb phrase is always *is*, *are*, *was*, or *were*. The subject in the last exercise is plural (*kittens*), so the helping verb *are* or *were* is required. The instructions say to use the verb *are*, so the sentence describes a present activity. If the helping verb *were* was used, then a past situation would be described.

Present: The kittens *are* drinking the milk

Past: The kittens *were* drinking the milk

But *be* is never used as a helping verb in such a progressive verb phrase. In each of the following exercises, you will correct an error by replacing *be* with *is*, *are*, *was*, or *were*.

EXERICES

1. Rewrite this sentence with *be* replaced by *is*.

   My sister Doris be taking five courses in college.

   _____

2. Rewrite this sentence with *be* replaced by *are*.

   Cities be building prisons instead of schools.

   _____

3. Rewrite this sentence with *be* replaced by *was*.

   Eugene be watching TV all morning.

   _____

4. Rewrite this sentence with *be* replaced by *were*.

The students be talking and laughing during the whole class, so I wrote a note to the principal asking him to attend the next class.

_____

CHAPTER

14

SPECIAL PEOPLE (*YOU* and *I*) WITH THE *BE* VERBS

For the past several chapters, we have been discussing a special family of verbs that includes *is*, *are*, *was*, and *were*. Also, Chapter 10 shows that *be* is the base form for this family of verbs. For convenience, grammarians refer to the entire family as "be verbs." We will refer to the group as *be*-verbs.

Special people (*you* and *I*) use special verb patterns with the *be*-verbs. These special patterns are discussed in this chapter.

Section I. Present Tense

We will begin with the present tense.

EXERCISES

Rewrite each of the following sentences with *is* in the blank space.

    1. James _____ a good friend.

_____

    2. My dog _____ a good friend.

_____

---

3. She _____ a good friend.

_____

The last three exercises show that for most singular subjects, the correct present tense *be*-verb is *is*. But the next exercise shows that when the subject is *you*, the correct *be*-verb is *are*.

EXERCISE

Rewrite this sentence with *is* replaced by *are*.

You is a good friend.

_____

The following sentence is incorrect.

WRONG: You *is* a good friend.

When the subject is *you*, the only correct present tense *be*-verb is *are*.

The next four exercises show a variety of sentences that all use *are* for the verb because *you* is the subject.

EXERCISES

Rewrite each sentence with *are* in the blank space.

1. You _____ kind and generous.

_____

2. You _____ a hard worker.

_____

3. You _____ in a lot of trouble.

_____

4. You _____ becoming a great cook.

_____

The subject *I* also employs a special pattern when used with the *be*-verb family. In fact, *I* uses a completely different member of the family. The next group of exercises concerns *I*.

EXERCISES

Rewrite each sentence with *is* in the blank space.

1. Richard _____ honest and reliable.

_____

2. My Aunt Marge _____ honest and reliable.

_____

3. She _____ honest and reliable.

_____

The last three exercises show that for most singular subjects, the correct present tense *be*-verb is *is*. But when the subject is *I*, the correct verb is *am*. This fact is shown in the next exercise.

EXERCISE

Rewrite this sentence with *am* in the blank space.

I _____ honest and reliable.

_____

The verb *am* is a very special verb. It is not used with any other subject except *I*. Yet it is the only correct verb to use with *I* when a sentence requires a *be*-verb.

The next four exercises show a variety of sentences that all use *am* as the verb because *I* is the subject.

EXERCISES

Rewrite each sentence with *am* in the blank space.

    1. I _____ always happy to help friends.

_____

    2. I _____ a fan of professional tennis.

_____

    3. I _____ undecided about where to live.

_____

    4. I _____ in between my brother and sister in age.

_____

Section II. Past Tense

So far we have discussed the present tense *be*-verbs used with *you* or *I* as the subject. Now we will turn to the past tense. The correct past past tense *be*-verb for *you* is *were*. The correct past tense *be*-verb for *I* is *was*. These facts are shown in the following table.

	Present	**Past**
You	are	were
I	am	was

The next exercise shows that *were* is the correct past tense verb when *you* is the subject of a sentence.

EXERCISE

Rewrite this sentence with *he* replaced by *you* and *was* replaced by *were*.

    He was a good dancer.

_____

The answer for the last exercise shows that when *you* is the subject of a sentence, the correct past tense *be*-verb is *were*. The next six exercises show different types of sentences that all use *were* as the past tense *be*-verb when *you* is the subject.

EXERCISE

Rewrite each sentence so that it makes a statement about the past by replacing *are* with *were*.

1. You are too talkative during movies.

_____

2. You are an inspiration to young athletes.

_____

3. You are involved in too many projects.

_____

4. You are at a wonderful age for growing and learning.

_____

5. You are the tallest person in your class.

_____

6. You are supporting your whole family.

_____

When the subject of a sentence is *I*, the correct past tense *be*-verb is *was*. This is shown in the next exercise.

EXERCISE

Rewrite this sentence so it makes a statement about the past by replacing *am* with *was*.

I am proud of how much money our group collected to help the homeless.

_____

The next six exercises show a variety of sentences that all use *was* as the past tense *be*-verb when *I* is the subject.

EXERCISE

Rewrite each exercise with *am* replaced by *was* to make a statement about the past.

1. I am a member of our school's marching band.

_____

2. I am finishing breakfast while doing my math homework.

_____

3. I am tired and hungry.

_____

4. I am under my car changing the oil.

_____

5. I am fortunate to have a generous grandfather.

_____

6. I am the fastest runner on our relay team.

_____

15

NOUNS

This chapter is about nouns. You know that verbs can represent actions. Nouns are the type of words that represent things, including persons, places, and objects. Examples of nouns are *chair*, *boy*, *Charley*, and *Texas*.

EXERCISES

1. How many nouns are in the sentence below? _____

    Paul eats pretzels and drinks soda for lunch.

Write the nouns from the sentence.

_____

2. How many nouns are in the sentence below? _____

    Mary reads slowly but accurately.

Write the nouns from the sentence.

_____

In the second sentence, the only noun is *Mary*. *Reads* represents an action, so it is a verb. *Slowly* and *accurately* tell how Mary reads. They do not represent things, so they are not nouns. But nouns do not represent only simple things.

The words "attitude" and "freedom" are nouns. We fight for freedom the way we would fight for our car if someone tried to take it. We regard a freedom as something we own. Grammatically "freedom" is a noun.

Concrete and Abstract Nouns

A simple noun like *chair*, representing something you can see, feel, and touch, is called a "concrete noun." A noun like "freedom" that represents a complex idea is called an "abstract noun." There is no sharp break between an abstract and a concrete noun. But some nouns are obviously more abstract than others, as illustrated by the next exercise.

EXERCISE

Here are 10 nouns:

lake, equality, car, faith, liberty, shoe, radio, evil, hand, justice

Write the five concrete nouns under the heading *Concrete* and the five abstract nouns under the heading *Abstract*.

Concrete	Abstract

Noun or Verb?

Some words can be used as a noun or a verb, depending on the role they play in a sentence. A word's ability to be either a noun or a verb is shown in the next exercise.

EXERCISES

Here are two sentences containing the word *water*.

    Sentence A: Mr. Taylor sprays water on his lawn.

    Sentence B: Mr. Taylor waters his lawn.

1. Write the sentence in which *water* is used as a verb.

_____

2. Write the sentence in which *water* is used as a noun.

_____

Here is a grammatical analysis of Sentence A.

    <u>Mr. Taylor</u>   <u>sprays</u>   <u>water</u> on his lawn.
       Subject   Verb   Object

Since *water* is the object, it is a noun in this sentence.

Here is a grammatical analysis of Sentence B.

    <u>Mr. Taylor</u>   <u>waters</u>   <u>his lawn</u>.
       Subject   Verb   Object

In this sentence *water* is the verb. It names an activity. Some words rarely play more than one role in a sentence. *Freedom* is seldom, if ever, used as a verb. The related verb *free* is used instead.

EXERCISES

Here are two sentences containing the word *pilots*.

Sentence A: Pilots fly thousands of planes across the nation's sky.

Sentence B: Captain Taylor pilots his large plane smoothly and safely.

1. Write the sentence in which *pilots* is used as a verb.

_____

2. Write the sentence in which *pilots* is used as a noun.

_____

CHAPTER

16

PROPER NOUNS

Nouns fall into two categories: common nouns and proper nouns. A common noun represents a general category of things. The word *boy* is a common noun. A proper noun may represent a specific case. The name *Paul* is a proper noun.

EXERCISES

1. Here are five proper nouns. Copy the list in this form because you will use the list in the next exercise.

Proper Nouns

Holland Tunnel _____

Cindy _____

Chevrolet _____

Wal-Mart _____

Gibson _____

2. Here are five common nouns: *tunnel*, *woman*, *store*, *guitar*, *car*. In the blank after each proper noun that you copied, write one of these common nouns.

Some textbooks say that a proper noun represents one specific thing and therefore should be capitalized. Note that one of the proper nouns on the above list is *Holland Tunnel*. There is just one Holland Tunnel. So *Holland Tunnel* fits the the popular belief that a proper noun names just one specific thing.

However, *Cindy* is also on our list of proper nouns. But there are many girls and women named Cindy, so it is not true that a proper noun names just one item or object. Some proper nouns just name fewer things than common nouns. They are more specific. Because of such complications in trying to define a proper noun, we will not just tell you to capitalize the first letter of every proper noun. Instead, we will present some guidelines concerning the types of nouns that are capitalized.

EXERCISES

A. The first letters of people's names are capitalized.

  1. Rewrite the sentence below with the first letter of the names of people capitalized.

    carlos and danny cut down myra's dead trees.

B. The first letters of brand names are capitalized such as Pontiac (cars), Ivory (soap), and other such products.

  2. Rewrite the sentence below with the first letters of brand names capitalized.

    We bought baskins-robbins ice cream, nabisco chocolate cookies, and mountain dew soda for dinner.

C. The names of cities, states, countries, and bodies of water are capitalized.

  3. Rewrite the sentence below with the first letters of a city, a state, and a body of water capitalized.

    During our vacation, we visited sacramento, california, on our way to the pacific ocean.

D. Titles of government officials such as mayors, governors, and senators are capitalized if they appear before the official's name but not if they appear by themselves in a sentence.

  4. Rewrite the sentence below with the word *governor* capitalized in one place but not in the other.

    Every day last week governor Williams called a different governor in one of our neighboring states to discuss common problems.

CHAPTER

17

POSSESSIVE FORMS OF NOUNS

If Bob owns a bike, we refer to it as *Bob's bike*.

Bob's bike = the bike owned by Bob

The noun *Bob* followed by an apostrophe (') and an *s* is called the "possessive form of the noun."

Bob's = possessive form of *Bob*

In discussing the possessive forms of nouns, we will need to use the word *phrase*. A phrase is a group of related words. Two phrases are illustrated in the next exercise.

EXERCISES

1. Here are two phrases.

Paul's dog
the black dog

Copy the phrase that includes the possessive form of a noun.

_____

---

2. Copy the following four phrases in the arrangement shown so you can use them in the next exercise.

   A. the teacher's briefcase:

   _____

   B. the lady's gloves:

   _____

   C. Jane's skates:

   _____

   D. the carpenter's tools:

   _____

3. Here are four more phrases. Copy each phrase next to the phrase with the same meaning in the group of phrases you copied for Exercise 2.

   A. the skates belonging to Jane.
   B. the tools owned by the carpenter
   C. the gloves belonging to the lady
   D. the briefcase owned by the teacher.

4. Rewrite the following sentence with the underlined phrases replaced by a phrase that contains a possessive form of a noun.

   <u>The tools owned by the carpenter</u> were stolen from his truck.

   _____

The underlined phrase can be replaced by this one:

   the carpenter's tools

Here is the answer.

   The carpenter's tools were stolen from his truck.

5. Rewrite the following sentence with the underlined phrase replaced by a phrase containing the possessive form of a noun.

The gloves belonging to the lady match her purse and shoes.

_____

6. Rewrite the following sentence with the underlined phrase replaced by a phrase containing the possessive form of a noun.

The briefcase owned by the teacher is full of papers that must be graded.

_____

7. Rewrite the following sentence with the underlined phrase replaced by a phrase containing the possessive form of a noun.

The house owned by Mr. Smith was damaged by a windstorm.

_____

Here is the answer.

Mr. Smith's house was damaged by a windstorm.

8. Rewrite the following sentence with the underlined phrase replaced by a phrase containing the possessive form of a noun.

The dog owned by Paul looks sad.

_____

9. Rewrite the following sentence with the underlined phrase replaced by a phrase containing the possessive form of a noun.

The car owned by Martin has been repaired.

_____

10. Rewrite the following sentence with the underlined phrase replaced by a phrase that contains the possessive form of a noun.

The instruments belonging to the doctor have been sterilized.

_____

The possessive form of a plural noun ending in *s* (such as *boys*) is created by adding an apostrophe after the *s*. For example, suppose several boys together bought a motorcycle. We could say it is the motorcycle owned by the boys. The next exercise shows how to express this idea with a phrase containing the possessive form of a noun.

EXERCISE

Rewrite this sentence with an apostrophe added after the *s* in the underlined word.

The motorcycle owned by the boys is the <u>boys</u> motorcycle.

_____

The answer for the last exercise shows that the motorcyle owned by several boys is the boys' motorcycle.

the boys' motorcycle = the motorcycle owned by several boys

EXERCISES

In each exercise, rewrite the sentence with an apostrophe added after the underlined word.

1. The room shared by two sisters is the <u>girls</u> room.

_____

2. We have three cats, and the small, swinging door they use to go in and out of the house is the <u>cats</u> door.

_____

Incidentally, if we had just one cat, then the door would be the *cat's* door.

the cats' door = the door used by several cats

the cat's door = the door used by one cat

Finally, let us consider plural nouns that do not end with an *s*, such as *children, women, mice,* and *men.* The posssessive form of such a noun is created by adding an apostrophe and an *s* at the end of the noun.

EXERCISE

Rewrite this sentence with an apostrophe and an *s* added to the underlined word.

The toys owned by several children are the <u>children</u> toys.

_____

The answer for the last exercise shows the following:

the children's toys = the toys owned by several children

EXERCISES

Rewrite each sentence with an apostrophe and an *s* added to the underlined word.

1. If several women bought a cabin by a lake for their families to use on vacations, it could be referred to as the <u>women</u> cabin.

_____

2. If the three children in a family have a TV which only they use, it could be referred to as the <u>children</u> TV.

_____

CHAPTER

ADDING ADJECTIVES TO SENTENCES

This chapter is about adjectives. Adjectives are words used to describe things.

EXERCISES

Here are two sentences.

Sentence A: Fred owns a car.
Sentence B: Fred owns a blue car.

Write the word that appears in Sentence B but not in Sentence A. _____

The answer for the last exercise is *blue*. *Blue* describes the car. So *blue* is an adjective.

EXERCISES

Here is a sentence with two adjectives.

A large cat chased a small dog.

1. Copy the sentence.

_____

2. Write the word *verb* under the verb. Write the word *noun* under each noun.

3. Write the word *adjective* under each adjective.

Here is the answer.

A   large   cat   chased   a   small   dog.
       Adjective   Noun   Verb   Adjective   Noun

To describe something, an adjective can be placed before the noun that names that thing.

EXERCISE

Rewrite Sentence A with the adjective from Sentence B right in front of the thing it describes.

Sentence A: We ate the strawberries for lunch.
Sentence B: The strawberries were delicious.

_____

The adjective in Sentence B is *delicious*. It describes the strawberries. Therefore, *delicious* is placed before the noun *strawberries* in Sentence A.

We ate the delicious strawberries for lunch.

EXERCISE

Rewrite Sentence A with the adjective from Sentence B right in front of the thing it describes.

Sentence A: We waded in the pool after dinner.
Sentence B: The pool was cool.

_____

The adjective in Sentence B is *cool*. It describes the pool. Therefore, *cool* is placed before the noun *pool* in Sentence A.

> We waded in the cool pool after dinner.

EXERCISE

Rewrite Sentence A with the adjective from Sentence B right in front of the thing it describes.

Sentence A: We warmed our hands before the fire.
Sentence B: The fire was hot.

_____

The adjective in Sentence B is *hot*. It describes the fire. Therefore, *hot* is placed before the noun *fire* in Sentence A.

> We warmed our hands before the hot fire.

If there is more than one noun in a sentence, an adjective can be added before each noun.

EXERCISE

Rewrite Sentence A with the adjectives from the other sentences placed before the appropriate nouns.

Sentence A: A writer must write a book.
Sentence B: The writer is successful.
Sentence C: The book is interesting.

_____

In the last exercise, according to Sentence B, the writer is successful. Therefore, *successful* can be written before *writer* in Sentence A. According to Sentence C, the book is interesting. Therefore, *interesting* can be written before *book* in Sentence A.

Here is the answer.

> A successful writer must write an interesting book.

EXERCISE

Rewrite Sentence A with the adjectives from the other sentences placed before the appropriate nouns.

   Sentence A: The roads caused a closing of schools.
   Sentence B: The roads were icy.
   Sentence C: The closing was early.

According to Sentence B of the last exercise, the roads were icy. Therefore, *icy* can be written before *roads* in Sentence A. According to Sentence C, the closing was early. Therefore, *early* can be written before *closing* in Sentence A.

Here is the answer:

   The icy roads caused an early closing of schools.

EXERCISE

Rewrite Sentence A with the adjectives from the other sentences placed before the appropriate nouns.

   Sentence A: Brock quickly got lost in the forest with trails.
   Sentence B: The forest was thick.
   Sentence C: The trails were unmarked.

Here is the answer:

   Brock quickly got lost in the thick forest with unmarked trails.

Here is a sentence containing the adjective *red*.

   The *red* shirt needs to be washed.

The adjective *red* describes the shirt. Grammarians say that the adjective *red* "modifies" the noun *shirt*. In grammar, the term *modify* means "add information to." The adjective *red* adds information to the noun *shirt*.

Grammarians say that an adjective "modifies" a noun because it changes or modifies a person's knowledge of the thing named by the noun. If you are told, "Sam bought a box of candy," you might think of the candy as just the ordinary sweet treat. But if you are told, "The candy is expensive," this information would change or "modify" your image of the candy.

You will see the term "modify" often in this book and other grammar books. Just remember that a modifier adds information to the word it modifies.

EXERCISES

1. What word do grammarians use to mean "add information"? _____

2. Copy this sentence with *modifies* in the blank.

   The adjective red _____ the noun shirt.

   _____

3. Rewrite the first sentence with the adjectives from the other sentences placed before the appropriate nouns.

   When it started to rain, a cat and a dog jumped into the window of your car.
   The cat is black.
   The dog is small.
   The window is open.
   The car is new.

   _____

4. Rewrite the first sentence with the adjectives from the other sentences placed before the appropriate nouns.

   The hikers ate the berries and drank the water from a mountain stream.
   The hikers were hungry.
   The berries were sweet.
   The water was pure.

   _____

5. Rewrite the first sentence with the adjectives from the other sentences place before the nouns they modify.

   Just before bedtime at summer camp, our counselor told us stories about events that happened in the woods on nights, like most of our nights.
   The counselor was devilish.
   The stories were scary.
   The events were horrible.
   The nights were dark.

   _____

MODIFYING ONE NOUN WITH TWO ADJECTIVES

If two adjectives modify the same noun, they can be placed before the noun. Generally a comma is placed between the adjectives.

EXERCISE

In Sentence A, the noun *horses* is underlined. In Sentences B and C, adjectives that modify *horses* are also underlined.

Rewrite Sentence A with the underlined adjectives from Sentences B and C placed before the noun *horses*.

Sentence A: The <u>horses</u> trotted onto the track.
Sentence B: The horses were <u>proud</u>.
Sentence C: The horses were <u>muscular</u>.

Since both adjectives modify the noun *horses*, they can both be placed before *horses*. Here is the answer.

The proud, muscular horses trotted onto the track.

EXERCISES

In each exercise, rewite Sentence A with the adjectives from the other sentences placed before the noun they modify. Place a comma between each pair of adjectives.

1. Sentence A: The display of fireworks at Miller Park fascinated the children.
   Sentence B: The display was loud.
   Sentence C: The display was dazzling.

   _____

2. Sentence A: My cat became an excellent mother.
   Sentence B: My cat is gentle.
   Sentence C: My cat is affectionate.

   _____

3. Sentence A: The sack held sandwiches, an apple, and a diamond ring.
   Sentence B: The sack was brown.
   Sentence C: The sack was wrinkled.

   _____

4. Sentence A: Their vacation had come to an end.
   Sentence B: The vacation was long.
   Sentence C: The vacation was carefree.

   _____

5. Sentence A: A Siamese won over all other breeds of cats at the show.
   Sentence B: The Siamese was blue-eyed.
   Sentence C: The Siamese was adorable.

   _____

CHAPTER

20

MODIFYING A NOUN WITH ANOTHER NOUN

Sometimes a noun is used to modify another noun. One noun is placed before another noun in a sentence.

EXERCISE

Rewrite Sentence A with the underlined noun from Sentence B placed before *bread*.

Sentence A: Kelly bakes bread.
Sentence B: A main ingredient is a <u>carrot</u>.

_____

The underlined noun in Sentence B is *carrot*. So *carrot* must be placed before *bread* in Sentence A. The answer to the exercise is below.

Kelly bakes carrot bread.

EXERCISES

In each exercise rewrite Sentence A with the underlined noun from Sentence B placed before the underlined noun in Sentence A.

1. Sentence A: John stirred <u>chips</u> into the cooky dough.
   Sentence B: The chips were made of <u>chocolate</u>.

   _____

2. Sentence A: Dad likes applesauce on his <u>pancake</u>.
   Sentence B: The main ingredient in the pancake is a big <u>potato</u>.

   _____

3. Sentence A: The children dance around the <u>tree</u>.
   Sentence B: The tree celebrates <u>Christmas</u>.

   _____

A regular adjective and a noun together can modify a noun in a sentence.

EXERCISE

Rewrite Sentence A with the adjective from Sentence B and the underlined noun from Sentence C placed before the underlined noun in Sentence A.

   Sentence A: We built a <u>wall</u> around our house.
   Sentence B: The wall is <u>circular</u>.
   Sentence C: The wall is made of <u>glass</u>.

   _____

The adjective in Sentence B is *circular*, so it can be placed before *wall* in Sentence A. The underlined noun in Sentence C is *glass*. A modifying noun like *glass* is generally placed closer to the modified noun (*wall*) than an adjective like *circular*. Here is the answer:

   We built a circular glass wall around our house.

Note that there is no comma between *circular* and *glass*. When an adjective and a noun are used to modify a noun, a comma is generally not placed between them.

EXERCISES

In each exercise, rewrite Sentence A with the adjective from Sentence B and the underlined noun from Sentence C in front of the underlined noun in Sentence A. Do not place a comma between the adjective and the noun.

1. Sentence A: We attended a <u>performance</u> of "Stars on Ice."
   Sentence B: The performance was <u>wonderful</u>.
   Sentence C: The performance was in the <u>afternoon</u>.

   _____

2. Sentence A: Ronald's class rode a <u>bus</u> to the game.
   Sentence B: The bus was <u>yellow</u>.
   Sentence C: The bus belonged to his <u>school</u>.

   _____

3. Sentence A: The <u>signals</u> were set for 30 miles an hour.
   Sentence B: The signals were <u>automated</u>.
   Sentence C: The signals controlled <u>traffic</u>.

   _____

4. Sentence A: Our team competed in a <u>tournament</u> last night.
   Sentence B: The tournament was <u>regional</u>.
   Sentence C: The tournament involved <u>basketball</u>.

   _____

21

PLACING TWO ADJECTIVES AFTER THE NOUN THEY MODIFY

Sometimes two adjectives can be placed after the noun they modify. This pattern is illustrated in the following exercise.

EXERCISE

Rewrite this sentence with *soft and warm* placed right after *bed*. Enclose the inserted words in commas.

My bed felt wonderful.

Here is the answer for the last exercise.

My bed, soft and warm, felt wonderful.

Commas

Note the commas enclosing the adjectives. Also note that the adjectives are joined by *and*.

EXERCISE

Rewrite Sentence A with the underlined phrase from Sentence B placed after *chicken* and enclosed in commas.

Sentence A: Mother's fried chicken is my favorite picnic snack.

Sentence B: The chicken is <u>crisp and spicy</u>.

_____

In the last exercise, Sentence B says the chicken is crisp and spicy. These adjectives can be placed after the noun *chicken* that they modify.

Mother's fried chicken, crisp and spicy, is my favorite picnic snack.

The next exercise illustrates a variation of this sentence pattern. The adjectives involved form somewhat of a contrast. Therefore, they are joined with *but* instead of *and*.

EXERCISE

Rewrite Sentence A with the underlined phrase from Sentence B placed after *car* and enclosed in commas.

Sentence A: My brother's car gets him to work every day.

Sentence B: My brother's car is <u>old but reliable</u>.

_____

Here is the answer for the last exercise.

My brother's car, old but reliable, gets him to work every day.

EXERCISE

Rewrite Sentence A with two adjectives from Sentence B placed after the noun that they modify. Join the adjectives with *and* and enclose them with commas.

Sentence A: My little sister's teddy bear is her favorite toy.

Sentence B: My little sister's teddy bear is tattered and torn.

_____

90

Sentence B presents two adjectives modifying *teddy bear*. These adjectives can be placed after *bear* in Sentence A.

My little sister's teddy bear, tattered and torn, is her favorite toy.

EXERCISES

1. Rewrite Sentence A with two adjectives from Sentence B placed right after the noun they modify. Join the adjectives with *and* and enclose them with commas.

   Sentence A: Grandfather's smile makes me feel comfortable at his house.
   Sentence B: Grandfather's smile is warm and welcoming.

   _____

2. Rewrite Sentence A with the adjectives from Sentence B (joined by *and*) placed after the noun they modify and enclosed in commas.

   Sentence A: Aunt Esther's fudge is a delightful Halloween treat.
   Sentence B: The fudge is soft and sweet.

   _____

CHAPTER

22

EXPRESSING COMPARISONS WITH ADJECTIVES

PART 1: USING *ER* TO EXPRESS THE OUTCOME OF A COMPARISON

Suppose you compare two people in height. You can use a special form of the adjective *tall* to state the outcome of your comparison. The special form is created by simply adding *er* to *tall*, as shown in the next exercise.

EXERCISE

Rewrite the sentence below with *er* added to *tall*.

> Sheri is *tall* than Bill.

Here is the answer.

> Sheri is *taller* than Bill.

Taller is called the comparative form of *tall* because it is used in stating the result of a comparison of two people or objects.

EXERCISES

1. Rewrite the sentence below with the comparative form of *fast*.

Air transportation is usually ___ than ground (car, bus, and train) transportation.

_____

The comparative form of *fast* is created by adding *er* to *fast*.

Here is the answer.

Air transportation is usually *faster* than ground (car, bus, and train) transportation.

2. Rewrite the sentence below with the *er* form of *small* in the blank.

Kittens are ___ than adult cats.

_____

PART 2: USING *MORE* TO FORM COMPARISONS

Long adjectives with 3 or more syllables do not use *er* to create the comparative form. Instead, *more* is placed in front of the adjective.

EXERCISE

Rewrite the sentence below with *more* inserted before *popular*.

Roses are *popular* than tulips.

_____

The adjective *popular* has 3 syllables. Adding *er* to the end of *popular* would be awkward. You can see the awkwardness by trying to pronounce the word formed by adding *er* to *popular*: *popularer*. Therefore, the comparative form of *popular* is formed by writing *more* in front of the adjective.

Here is the answer for the last exercise.

Roses are *more* popular than tulips.

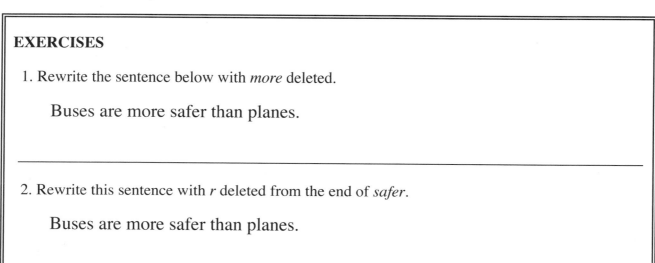

EXERCISES

In each exercise, rewrite the sentence with *more* placed before the underlined adjective.

1. A Lincoln Town Car is <u>expensive</u> than a Ford Crown Victoria, although the latter automobile is about as large and powerful.

   _____

2. A Lincoln Town Car is <u>luxurious</u> than a Ford Crown Victoria, which is the main reason for the Lincoln's greater cost.

   _____

PART 3: AVOIDING DOUBLE COMPARATIVE FORMS

What is wrong with this sentence?

   Buses are more safer than planes.

The sentence uses both comparative forms of the adjective *safe*. *More* is written before *safe*, and *er* is written at the end of *safe*. The result sounds awkward and is redundant (repeats itself). The next exercises show two ways to correct this error.

EXERCISES

1. Rewrite the sentence below with *more* deleted.

   Buses are more safer than planes.

   _____

2. Rewrite this sentence with *r* deleted from the end of *safer*.

   Buses are more safer than planes.

   _____

The answers for the last two exercises show that for some shorter adjectives with one or two syllables, the comparative form may be constructed in one of two ways: *more* can be placed in front of the adjective, or *er* can be placed at the end.

94

PART 4: USING *EST* TO FORM SUPERLATIVES

To indicate that one object has more of a characteristic named by an adjective than any other object, the *est* form of the adjective is used.

EXERCISE

Rewrite the sentence below with *est* added to *long*.

Omar is the long snake in our zoo.

_____

The *est* form of *long* is *longest*.

So here is the answer.

Omar is the *longest* snake in our zoo.

The *est*-form of an adjective is called the "superlative" form. "Superlative" contains the word *super* which is also found in *Superman* and *supermarket*. "Super" means biggest or best.

EXERCISE

Rewrite this sentence with *comparative* in one blank and *superlative* in the other.

The _____ form of an adjective is used to describe the result of comparing two objects, whereas the _____ form of an adjective is used to describe the result of comparing three or more objects to see which has the most of the characteristic named by the adjective.

_____

PART 5: USING *MOST* TO FORM SUPERLATIVES

The adjective *expensive* contains three syllables. Adding *est* at the end would be awkward. Therefore, *most* is written in front.

Here is the correct answer.

This brooch contains the most expensive diamond in the world.

If an adjective has three or more syllables, then the superlative form is not created by adding *est*. Instead, the word *most* is placed in front of the adjective. The answer for the next exercise presents another illustration of a superlative adjective constructed with *most*.

Here is the answer for the last exercise.

The *most beautiful* senior girl became a movie star.

The phrase *most beautiful* is considered the superlative form of the adjective *beautiful*. The final exercise in this section provides one more example of a superlative adjective.

EXERCISE

Rewrite this sentence with the underlined adjective in its superlative form.

The <u>valuable</u> pro basketball player in the All-Star game won a million dollar bonus.

_____

The answer to the last exercise shows that the superlative form of *valuable* is *most valuable*.

PART 6: USING *ANY* AND *ANY OTHER* CORRECTLY

People often make a certain type of error when discussing the results of a comparison. What is wrong with this statement?

Tom is taller than every boy in his class.

Tom is not taller than himself. So he is not taller than every boy in his class. We can only say that Tom is taller than every *other* boy in his class.

EXERCISES

Rewrite each sentence with *other* inserted after any.

1. I am older than any member of my algebra class.

_____

2. Geri's horse is better trained than any horse in her riding class.

_____

23

ADVERBS THAT DESCRIBE AN ACTION AND END IN -*LY*

Adverbs are a large group of words. They can be used to convey various types of information, such as how an action is performed. This use is illustrated in the next exercise.

EXERCISE

Rewrite this sentence with *silently* placed after *crept*.

> The lion crept towards its prey.

_____

The verb in the sentence, (*crept*) describes the action of the lion. The adverb *silently* describes how the action is done.

Here is the answer.

> The lion crept *silently* towards its prey.

EXERCISE

Rewrite this sentence with the adverb *gleefully* placed before the verb *opened*.

Gilbert opened his birthday gift.

_____

The adverb *gleefully* describes how Gilbert opened his birthday gift.

Here is the correct answer.

Gilbert gleefully opened his birthday gift.

Here are the two adverbs used in the last two exercises

silently   gleefully

Note that both end in *ly*. Most adverbs that tell how actions occur end in *ly*.

A few adverbs that tell how actions occur do not end in *ly*. And a few English words ending in *ly* are not adverbs, such as *belly*.

But most words that end in *ly* are adverbs that tell how an action occurs. For example, *quickly*, *sadly*, and *carefully* are all adverbs.

The next three exercises illustrate three more adverbs that end in *ly* and tell how an action occurred.

EXERCISES

1. Rewrite this sentence with the adverb *happily* placed before the verb *licked*.

Little Suzie *licked* the cake frosting bowl clean.

_____

2. Rewrite this sentence with the adverb *joyfully* placed before the verb *rolled*.

Our dog Spot *rolled* in the dust.

_____

3. Rewrite this sentence with the adverb *fearfully* placed before the verb *handed*.

My brother Albert *handed* Father his report card.

_____

24

MOVING ADVERBS

Some adverbs can be placed in more than one position in a sentence as shown by the next exercise.

EXERCISE

Rewrite this sentence with the adverb *joyfully* moved to the end of the sentence.

Lisa skipped *joyfully* into the kitchen.

_____

Here is the answer for the last exercise.

Lisa skipped into the kitchen joyfully.

Note that in the original sentence *joyfully* is placed after the verb *skipped*. The adverb could also be placed in front of the verb.

Lisa *joyfully* skipped into the kitchen.

Finally, the adverb could be placed at the beginning of the sentence.

Joyfully, Lisa skipped into the kitchen.

Notice that *joyfully* is set off with a comma in the last sentence. An adverb at the beginning of a sentence is often set off with a comma.

EXERCISES

1. Rewrite this sentence with the adverb *successfully* moved to the end of the sentence.

   The daredevil *successfully* climbed the highest building in town.

   _____

2. Rewrite this sentence by placing the adverb *luckily* at the beginning of the sentence. Remember to put a comma after the adverb.

   Ann *luckily* found her lost purse.

   _____

3. Rewrite this sentence by placing the adverb *encouragingly* after the verb *spoke*.

   Encouragely, the teacher spoke to her class before their reading test.

   _____

4. Rewrite this sentence by placing the adverb *favorably* at the end of the sentence.

   Brian wrote *favorably* of his new soccer coach.

   _____

5. Rewrite this sentence by placing the adverb *surprisingly* at the beginning of the sentence. Put a comma after the beginning adverb.

   Great Grandmother *surprisingly* praised Debbie's first pie.

   _____

CHAPTER

25

ADVERBS MODIFYING ADJECTIVES

Sometimes the main purpose of an adverb in a sentence is to modify an adjective. You will add such an adverb to a sentence in the next exercise.

EXERCISE

Rewrite this sentence with the adverb *astonishingly* placed before the adjective *strong*.

Monkeys are strong for their size.

_____

Here is the answer for this exercise.

Monkeys are <u>astonishingly</u>   <u>strong</u> for their size.
                     Adverb   Adjective

The adverb *astonishingly* modifies the adjective *strong*. Adverbs that modify adjectives are generally placed right before the adjective. This type of adverb cannot be moved around the way adverbs that modify verbs can be.

Two common adverbs that modify adjectives are *very* and *too*. Their use is illustrated in the exercises below.

EXERCISE

Rewrite this sentence by placing *very* before *salty*.

This popcorn is salty.

_____

Here is the answer to this exercise.

This popcorn is <u>very</u>   <u>salty</u>.
               Adverb   Adjective

In the original sentence, the popcorn is called "salty." It may be salty but still an enjoyable treat. However, in the answer, the popcorn is called "very salty," a degree of saltiness beyond "salty." In fact, it may be too salty to eat. The word "too" is used as an adverb to mean "very" or "exceedingly." *Too* is used with that meaning in the next exercise.

EXERCISE

Rewrite this sentence by placing *too* before *short*.

This dress is short in Mother's opinion.

_____

Here is the answer to the last exercise.

This dress is <u>too</u>   <u>short</u>   in Mother's opinion.
            Adverb   Adjective

In this exercise, the adverb *too* describes the degree of shortness of the dress. In Mother's opinion, it is not just "short" but "too short" and not suitable to wear in public. Many *ly* adverbs may also be used to describe adjectives as illustrated in the exercises below.

EXERCISES

1. Rewrite this sentence by placing *exceedingly* before *sour*.

This lemonade is sour.

_____

2. Rewrite this sentence by placing *hilariously* before *funny*.

The new TV cartoon series is funny.

_____

3. Rewrite this sentence by placing *remarkably* before *generous*.

The leg room in the new Texas Airlines economy seats is generous.

_____

4. Rewrite this sentence by placing *uncharacteristically* before *short*.

John Paul Jones, U. S. Navy hero of the Revolutionary War, was short for a captain who excelled in fierce hand-to-hand combat.

_____

26

OTHER TYPES OF ADVERBS

Some adverbs do not end with *ly*. Nor do they tell how an action occurs. Instead, they tell *when*, *where*, *how often*, and *how long* the action takes place.

EXERCISE

Rewrite this sentence with *often* before *eats*.

Irene eats French toast for breakfast.

_____

Here is the answer.

Irene *often* eats French toast for breakfast.

The adverb *often* tells how *frequently* the action occurs (how frequently Irene eats French toast for breakfast). Other adverbs are illustrated by the following exercises.

EXERCISES

1. Rewrite this sentence with *never* placed before *eats*.

   Sally eats spinach.

   _____

2. Rewrite this sentence with *sometimes* placed at the beginning of the sentence.

   Dan goes to stockcar races.

   _____

3. Rewrite this sentence with *upstairs* placed at the end of the sentence.

   Grandfather hid some Easter eggs.

   _____

4. Rewrite this sentence with *never* before *arrives*.

   Mae arrives on the 5 p.m. bus.

   _____

5. Rewrite this sentence with *soon* at the beginning of the sentence.

   Cyrus will be old enough to drive.

   _____

Most single words that express information about time or place in a sentence are adverbs.

CHAPTER

27

PREPOSITIONS: USING PREPOSITIONAL PHRASES TO MODIFY NOUNS

What is wrong with this sentence?

Carl fell asleep after spending all day skiing on the train.

EXERCISE

Rewrite the above sentence to eliminate the problem.

_____

The problem with the sentence above is that the phrase "on the train" is misplaced. Carl did not ski *on the train*. This phrase should be placed after *asleep*.

Here is the answer.

Carl fell asleep *on the train* after spending all day skiing.

"On the train" is called a "prepositional phrase." This chapter is about prepositions and prepositional phrases. Generally, prepositions are short common words like the following: *on*, *in*, *at*, *of*, and *by*.

A preposition is usually followed by a noun. The noun is called the "object" of the preposition. The preposition and the noun together form a prepositional phrase.

Here is a prepositional phrase.

prepositional phrase

on the train

Preposition   Object of Preposition

A phrase is a group of words that form a meaningful unit in a sentence.

A prepositional phrase can be used to provide various types of information. This next exercise shows how a prepositional phrase can be used to provide information about the location of something.

Here is the answer for the last exercise.

The multi-colored bird *in the window* costs $500.

The prepositional phrase helps identify which bird costs $500 and where it is located.

In the last exercise, the prepositional phrase is placed right after *bird* because it provides information about the bird. In grammatical terminology, such a prepositional phrase is said to modify the noun *bird* because it provides additional information about the bird. The next exercise presents another example of a prepositional phrase that modifies a noun.

EXERCISE

Rewrite Sentence A with the prepositional phrase placed after *man*.

Sentence A: The man is my basketball coach.

Prepositional Phrase: with the crewcut

The prepositional phrase *with the crewcut* is placed right after the noun *man* because it provides additional information about the man.

Here is the answer.

The man with the crewcut is my basketball coach.

To modify a noun, a prepositional phrase is placed right after the noun. This is illustrated in the exercises you have done. For example, in the last exercise, *with the crewcut* is placed after *man*. This principle is shown again in the next exercise.

EXERCISE

Rewrite Sentence A with the prepositional phrase inserted after *house*.

Sentence A: The old, deserted house is haunted.

Prepositional Phrase: by the cemetery

In order to modify *house*, the prepositional phrase "by the cemetery" must be placed right after *house*.

Here is the answer.

The old, deserted house by the cemetery is haunted.

Additional examples of prepositional phrases modifying nouns are provided by the following exercises.

EXERCISES

1. Rewrite Sentence A with the prepositional phrase placed after *cat*.

   Sentence A: The cat belongs to my sister.
   Prepositional Phrase: under your car

   _____

2. Rewrite Sentence A with the prepositional phrase placed after *bus*.

   Sentence A: The bus will arrive about an hour late.
   Prepositional Phrase: from Chicago

   _____

3. Rewrite Sentence A with the prepositional phrase placed after *cheeseburger*.

   Sentence A: Wendy ordered a cheeseburger for lunch.
   Prepositional Phrase: with lettuce, a tomato slice, and mayonaise

   _____

4. Rewrite Sentence A with the prepositional phrase placed right after *gift*.

   Sentence A: The world-class sprinter's shoes were a gift.
   Prepositional Phrase: from Nike

   _____

5. Rewrite Sentence A with the prepositional phrase placed after *World*.

   Sentence A: Anita's birthday present was a trip to Disney World.
   Prepositional Phrase: in Orlando, Florida

   _____

6. Rewrite Sentence A with the prepositional phrase placed after *can*.

   Sentence A: Sally opened a small can to have for dessert.
   Prepositional Phrase: of sliced peaches

   _____

In this chapter, you have worked with the following prepositions: *after, by, from, in, on, of, under,* and *with*.

Here are some other common prepositions: *about, above, across, against, along, among, around, as, at, before, behind, below, beneath, beside, besides, between, beyond, by, concerning, down, during, inside, into, like, off, next, onto, out, outside, over, past, regarding, since, through, throughout, underneath, unlike, up, upon, with, within,* and *without.*

It is not necessary to memorize this list. In time you will easily recognize prepositional phrases. Generally, they provide five kinds of information:

Location	Time	Origin	Destination	Comparision
in the house	after dinner	from China	to Chicago	like lost sheep

28

PREPOSITIONAL PHRASES THAT PROVIDE INFORMATION ABOUT ACTIONS AND EVENTS

Some prepositional phrases do not provide information about nouns. Instead they provide information about the events or situations described in sentences. Two such prepositional phrases are illustrated in the next exercise.

EXERCISE

Rewrite Sentence A with the prepositional phrases at the end of the sentence.

Sentence A: My car was stolen.
Prepositional Phrase: from the parking lot
Prepositional Phrase: on Monday night

Sentence A describes an event. The prepositional phrases beneath the sentence give additional information about the event.

In the last chapter, the prepositional phrases provide additional information about a specific noun. They modify nouns. In this sense, they are somewhat like adjectives. Therefore, they are adjectival. But the prepositional phrases in the last exercise do not provide information about a specific noun. Instead, they provide information about an action or event. In this sense, they are somewhat like adverbs, and they are called adverbial.

Here is the answer for the last exercise.

My car was stolen from the parking lot on Monday night.

EXERCISE

Rewrite Sentence A with the prepositional phrases at the end.

Sentence A: I bought a beautiful blue suit.
Prepositional Phrase: during my trip
Prepositional Phrase: to Chicago

Here is the answer for the last exercise.

I bought a beautiful blue suit during my trip to Chicago.

Prepositional phrases can add many types of information to a sentence, as illustrated by the remaining exercises.

EXERCISES

1. Rewrite Sentence A with the prepositional phrases at the end.

Sentence A: Gilbert takes saxophone lessons every Thursday.
Prepositional Phrase: from a professional saxophonist
Prepositional Phrase: in a rehearsal hall

_____

2. Rewrite Sentence A with the prepositional phrases at the end.

Sentence A: Amy does homework every evening.
Prepositional phrase: at the library
Prepositional phrase: near her home

_____

3. Rewrite Sentence A with the prepositional phrases at the end.

Sentence A: Cynthia served pumpkin pie and coffee.
Prepositional Phrase: after dinner
Prepositional Phrase: in the living room

_____

4. Rewrite Sentence A with the prepositional phrases at the end.

Sentence A: Tony plans to go ice skating.
Prepositional Phrase: at the skating rink
Prepositional Phrase: near the new movie theater.

_____

5. Rewrite Sentence A with the prepositional phrases at the end.

Sentence A: Lily wanted a leather coat.
Prepositonal Phrase: for her Alaskan trip
Prepositional Phrase: in the fall

_____

EXERCISE

Rewrite the following sentence with *adverbial* in one blank and *adjectival* in the other.

A prepositional phrase that modifies a specific noun is called _____ whereas a prepositional phrase that provides additional information about an action or event is called _____.

_____

29

PREPOSITIONAL PHRASES AT THE BEGINNINGS OF SENTENCES

Sometimes a prepositional phrase fits nicely at the beginning of a sentence, as shown in the next exercise.

EXERCISE

Rewrite this sentence with the underlined prepositional phrase moved to the front and set off with a comma.

Our teacher has us spend five minutes writing about our major goal for the day <u>at the beginning of each class</u>.

_____

Here is the answer for the last exercise.

At the beginning of each class, our teacher has us spend five minutes writing about our major goal for the day.

Note that the prepositional phrase is set off with a comma. Sometimes a short prepositional phrase at the beginning of a sentence need not be set off with a comma. But an initial prepositional phrase of four or more words is usually set off with a comma.

In the last exercise, the prepositional phrase concerns the beginning of an event. Therefore, the prepositional phrase itself seems to fit most naturally at the beginning of the sentence. In the next exercise, the prepositional phrase also concerns an activity that occurs at the beginning of a period of time. This prepositional phrase also seems to fit well at the beginning of the sentence.

EXERCISES

Rewrite each sentence with the underlined prepositional phrase moved to the front and set off with a comma.

1. The owner of the store where I work takes inventory <u>on the first day of each month</u> to determine exactly what merchandise he has on hand and what he needs to order.

_____

2. Many stores sell more merchandise <u>between Thanksgiving and Christmas</u> than they sell the rest of the year.

_____

Here is the answer for the last exercise.

> Between Thanksgiving and Christmas, many stores sell more merchandise than they sell the rest of the year.

In the last exercise, which sentence do you prefer, the original or the one with the prepositional phrase in front?

In some contexts, the original sentence might sound smoother or seem more appropriate. In these cases, the prepositional phrase should not be moved to the front.

EXERCISES

Rewrite each sentence with the underlined prepositional phrase moved to the front.

1. I have significantly reduced my blood pressure <u>by eliminating salt from my diet</u>.

_____

2. You are ready to begin connecting your new VCR to your TV <u>after reading the directions in the VCR manual carefully</u>.

_____

3. People have been experiencing difficulty getting enough food <u>throughout Eastern Europe</u>.

_____

Here is the answer for the last exercise.

> Throughout Eastern Europe people have been experiencing difficulty getting enough food.

Note that the prepositional phrase at the beginning is not set off with a comma. Since the prepositional phrase contains only three words, omitting the comma does not confuse readers.

CHAPTER

PREPOSITIONAL PHRASES THAT MODIFY OBJECTS IN OTHER PREPOSITIONAL PHRASES

A useful feature of prepositional phrases is that one prepositional phrase can modify the object of another prepositional phrase. This feature is illustrated in the next set of exercises.

We will start with this sentence.

I can repay your loan today if you meet me by the employees' lounge.

Then we will add a prepositional phrase that provides information about the employees' lounge.

EXERCISE

Rewrite Sentence A with the prepositional phrase at the end.

Sentence A: I can repay your loan today if you meet me by the employees' lounge.

Prepositional Phrase: in the Sears store

Next we will add a prepositional phrase that provides information about the location of the store.

EXERCISE

Rewrite Sentence B with the prepositional phrase at the end.

Sentence B: I can repay your loan today if you meet me by the employees' lounge in the Sears store.

Prepositional Phrase: at the new mall

Next we will add a prepositional phrase that provides information about the location of the mall.

EXERCISE

Rewrite Sentence C with the prepositional phrase at the end.

Sentence C: I can repay your loan today if you meet me by the employees' lounge in the Sears store at the new mall.

Prepositional Phrase: near the freeway

Finally, we will add a prepositional phrase that provides information about the freeway.

EXERCISE

Rewrite Sentence D with the prepositional phrase at the end.

Sentence D: I can repay your loan today if you meet me by the emloyees' lounge in the Sears store at the new mall near the freeway.

Prepositional Phrase: from New Jersey

Here is the answer.

I can repay your loan today if you meet me by the employees' lounge in the Sears store at the new mall off the freeway from New Jersey.

120

Chapter 26 discusses the use of prepositional phrases to modify nouns. Since the object of a prepositional phrase is generally a noun, using one prepositional phrase to modify the object of another prepositional phrase is just an application of this usage. However, repeating the pattern with several prepositional phrases allows various details of a situation to be decribed. The next exercise shows another example.

EXERCISE

Rewrite Sentence A with the prepositional phrases at the end, one after another.

Sentence A: The aliens left their space ship on the roof.

Prepositional Phrase: of a building

Prepositional Phrase: near my old apartment

Prepositional Phrase: in Greenwich Village

Here is the answer for the last exercise.

The aliens left their space ship on the roof of a building near my old apartment in Greenwich Village.

In this sentence, the prepositional phrase *near my old apartment* modifies *building* which is itself the object of a prepositional phrase. The last prepositional phrase *in Greenwich Village* modifies *apartment* which is also the object of a prepositional phrase.

The remaining exercises show additional examples of "chaining" together prepositional phrases by letting each successive prepositional phrase modify the object of the previous one.

EXERCISES

1. Rewrite Sentence A with the prepositional phrases at the end, one after another.

Sentence A: Ted is responsible for the error.

Prepositional Phrase: in the bill

Prepositional Phrase: of the customer

Prepositional Phrase: at Table 6

---

2. Rewrite Sentence A with the prepositional phrases at the end, one after another.

Sentence A: When I graduate, I can quit my job.

Prepositional Phrase: in the smelly meat department

Prepositional Phrase: of Bud's grocery store

Prepositional Phrase: behind the old shopping center

Prepositional Phrase: near your uncle's furniture factory

CHAPTER

31

SUBJECT-VERB AGREEMENT WITH AN INTERVENING PREPOSITIONAL PHRASE

When a prepositional phrase is placed between the subject and verb of a sentence, the verb does not change form.

EXERCISE

Here are two sentences that differ only in the form of their verbs.

The box of cookies *are* empty.

The box of cookies *is* empty.

Copy the correct sentence.

If you wrote the sentence with *is*, your answer is correct. The subject of the sentence (*box*) is singular, so the verb must also be singular (*is*). To see why *box* is considered the subject in this sentence, do the next exercise.

EXERCISE

Rewrite Sentence A with the underlined prepositional phrase from Sentence B placed right after the noun it modifies.

    Sentence A: The box is empty.
    Sentence B: It was a box <u>of cookies</u>.

Sentence A shows that the basic subject in the sentence is *box*. Sentence B shows that *of cookies* is a prepositional phrase that can be placed between the subject and the verb. But the subject is still considered to be *box*. Here is the answer.

    The   <u>box</u>   <u>of cookies</u>   <u>is</u> empty.
         Subject   Prepositional Phrase   Verb

Here is a similar exercise.

EXERCISE

Rewrite Sentence A with the underlined prepositional phrase from Sentence B placed right after the noun it modifies.

    Sentence A: The barrel is blocking shopping-cart traffic in Aisle 3.
    Sentence B: It is a barrel <u>of apples, oranges, and walnuts</u>.

Here is the combined sentence.

    The barrel of apples, oranges, and walnuts is blocking shopping-cart traffic in Aisle 3.

Inexperienced writers often use the verb *are* instead of *is* for a sentence such as this one. Because the plural words *apples, oranges, and walnuts* are closer to the verb than *barrel*, they choose a plural verb. Through practice, however, they learn to distinguish between a singular subject and an intervening prepositional phrase with plural objects. The next exercise is a little different.

The correct sentence in the last exercise is Sentence B. The subject of the sentence is *safety*. This singular subject is modified by a prepositional phrase with a plural object. The combination of subject and object can confuse a weak writer. Here is the answer.

The <u>safety</u> <u>of our troops in foreign countries</u> <u>is</u> under review.
       Subject   Prepositional Phrase   Verb

EXERCISES

In each exercise, copy the sentence with the correct form of the verb.

1. Sentence A: Only one person out of several hundred applicants were hired.
   Sentence B: Only one person out of several hundred applicants was hired.

2. Sentence A: A truck in one of our three parking lots are filled with explosives.
   Sentence B: A truck in one of our three parking lots is filled with explosives.

3. Sentence A: My monkey's favorite food for breakfast, lunch, dinner, or between-meal snacks are bananas.
   Sentence B: My monkey's favorite food for breakfast, lunch, dinner, or between-meal snacks is bananas.

32

COORDINATING CONJUNCTIONS: JOINING ENTIRE SENTENCES

This chapter is about conjunctions. Conjunctions are used to join words, phrases, or sentences together. For example, the conjunction *and* joins two nouns together in this phrase:

lettuce   and   tomatoes

Noun   Conjunction   Noun

EXERCISE

Write the term *conjunction*:

_____

There are two main types of conjunctions. This chapter discusses one type: the coordinating conjunction. Here are the six major coordinating conjunctions.

and	**so**
or	**for**
but	**yet**

EXERCISES

1. Write the term coordinating conjunction:

_____

2. Write six coordinating conjunctions:

_____

Coordinating conjunctions can be used for joining words, phrases, or entire sentences. This chapter discusses their use for joining entire sentences. The following exercise shows how the coordinating conjunction *and* can be used to join two sentences into one.

EXERCISE

Rewrite Sentence A, but replace the period with a comma. Then write *and*. Finally, write Sentence B but do not capitalize its first letter.

Sentence A: Brad mowed the lawn.
Sentence B: His daughter picked flowers.

_____

Here is the answer for the last exercise.

Brad mowed the lawn, and his daughter picked flowers.
↗
Comma

Note the comma before *and*. When two sentences are joined by a coordinating conjunction, a comma is generally placed before the coordinating conjunction.

Note also that the first letter in Sentence B is no longer capitalized. The *h* in *his* is not capitalized because Sentence B is no longer a separate sentence. It has become part of the longer combined sentence. Each coordinating conjunction has a different meaning. The conjunction *and* is used for joining two sentences that express similar ideas, so that the second sentence adds to the picture presented by the first one. The conjunction *and* is used again in the next exercise.

EXERCISE

Write Sentence A with the period replaced by a comma. Then write *and*. Finally, write Sentence B but do not capitalize its first letter.

    Sentence A: Lisa earned a degree in journalism from Columbia University.
    Sentence B: She has five years experience working as a reporter for the *New York Times*.

_____

Here is the answer for the last exercise.

> Lisa earned a degree in journalism from Columbia University, and she has five years experience working for the *New York Times*.

The following exercises illustrate the meanings of the other coordinating conjunctions.

BUT is used to signal a contrast between the ideas presented in two sentences

---

EXERCISE

Rewrite Sentence A with the period replaced by a comma. Then write *but*. Finally, write Sentence B but do not capitalize the first letter.

    Sentence A: Paul went to the refrigerator for a cold soda.
    Sentence B: The refrigerator was empty.

_____

The ideas in the sentences present somewhat of a contrast. The conjunction *but* is used to signal a contrast. So the sentences can be joined with *but*.

> Paul went to the refrigerator for a cold soda, but the refrigerator was empty.

The conjunction *OR* presents two choices

EXERCISE

Rewrite Sentence A with the period replaced by a comma. Then write *or*. Finally, rewrite Sentence B but do not capitalize the first letter.

    Sentence A: We could fix dinner at home tonight.
    Sentence B: We could try the new Chinese restaurant downtown.

_____

The conjunction *SO* presents a result or consequence

EXERCISE

Write Sentence A followed by a comma. Next write *so*. Finally, write Sentence B, but do not capitalize the first letter.

    Sentence A: Carl wanted to become a chemist.
    Sentence B: He took all of the science and math courses at his school.

_____

YET presents an idea that is unexpected in light of the previous sentence

Yet is somewhat like *but*. However, *yet* may be used when the second idea seems more unexpected or more inconsistent than in sentences using *but*.

EXERCISE

Rewrite Sentence A with the period replaced by a comma. Then write *yet*. Finally, write Sentence B but do not capitalize the first letter.

    Sentence A: Lisa never took singing lessons.
    Sentence B: She won a college vocal music scholarship.

_____

FOR presents a cause or reason for the situation or event just described

---

EXERCISE

Rewrite Sentence A with the period replaced by a comma. Then write *for*. Finally, write Sentence B but do not capitalize the first letter.

    Sentence A: Nick saved his spare change for a year.
    Sentence B: He planned to buy his mother a special birthday gift.

_____

When you combine two complete sentences into one sentence with a coordinating conjunction, you create a *compound sentence*. You created compound sentences in the last five exercises in this chapter.

EXERCISE

Write the term *compound sentence*:

_____

22

USING *AND* TO JOIN THE SUBJECTS OF SENTENCES WITH IDENTICAL PREDICATES

In a sentence such as the following, everything except the subject is called the predicate.

<u>Paul</u>   <u>plays tennis every afternoon</u>.
Subject   Predicate

EXERCISES

1. Copy this sentence:

    Children enjoy writing poetry.

_____

2. In the sentence you just wrote, underline the subject and write *subject* under it.

3. Underline the predicate and write *predicate* under it.

---

4. Copy this sentence:

   Adults enjoy writing poetry.

   _____

5. In the sentence you just copied, underline the subject and write *subject* under it.

6. Underline the predicate and write *predicate* under it.

Here are the two sentences you just copied and analyzed.

   Children enjoy writing poetry.

   Adults enjoy writing poetry.

Notice that the sentences have different subjects but identical predicates. These sentences can be combined with the conjunction *and* by following two steps:

   Step 1. Write the subjects of the sentences joined by the conjunction *and*.

   Step 2. Then write the predicate just once after the two subjects.

Following these steps with the above sentences produces the following answer:

   Children and adults   <u>enjoy writing poetry</u>.
                            Predicate

You can use these steps for the following exercises.

EXERCISE

Combine these sentences with the conjunction *and*.

   Sentence A: Humans need food to survive.
   Sentence B: Animals need food to survive.

   _____

The last exercise can be answered in two steps.

   Step 1: Write the subjects of the two sentences joined by *and*.

   Humans and animals

Step 2: Write the predicate just once after the two subjects.

Humans and animals <u>need food to survive</u>.
Predicate

Here is the answer for the last exercise.

Humans and animals need food to survive.

Note that there is no comma before *and*. Generally a comma is not needed if only parts of sentences are joined with *and*. A comma is used only when whole sentences are joined together. In the answer for the last exercise, the subject is called a compound subject.

<u>Humans and animals</u>   <u>need food to survive</u>.
Compound subject   Predicate

A compound subject formed with *and* is considered plural and requires a plural verb. Use this information in the next exercise.

EXERCISE

Combine these sentences by joining the subjects with *and* and then writing the predicate just once after the subject.

Sentence A: Pete likes wearing new clothes.
Sentence B: Petina likes wearing new clothes.

The last exercise can be answered in two steps:

1. The subjects are joined with *and*.

   Pete and Petina

2. The predicate is written just once after the subjects.

   Pete and Petina <u>like wearing new clothes</u>.
   Predicate

Here is the answer for the exercise.

Pete and Petina *like* wearing new clothes.

Note that the verb in the answer does not end in *s* because the compound subject is plural.

EXERCISES

1. Combine these two sentences into a single sentence with a compound subject.

Sentence A: Cindy goes trick or treating every Halloween.
Sentence B: Zach goes trick or treating every Halloween.

Here is the answer for the last exercise.

Cindy and Zach *go* trick or treating every Halloween.

In each of the original sentences, the verb has the singular form *goes*. But in the answer, the verb has the plural form *go*. The compound subject is plural. Therefore, it requires a plural verb. Use this information in answering the next exercise.

EXERCISE

Combine these two sentences into a single sentence with a compound subject.

Sentence A: Little Tommy jumps into puddles after rainstorms.
Sentence B: His dog Skamp jumps into puddles after rainstorms.

Chapter 26 discusses modifying nouns with prepositional phrases. If the subject of a sentence is modified by a prepositional phrase, the prepositional phrase is part of the complete subject, not part of the predicate. Use this idea in the next exercises.

EXERCISE

In the sentence below, the subject *apartments* is modified by the prepositional phrase *in New York*. Copy the sentence and underline the complete subject. Write *complete subject* under it. Then underline the predicate and write *predicate* under it.

Apartments in New York are terribly expensive.

Apartments in many areas of the country are not very expensive. It is only in New York City that apartments are almost unaffordable. The sentence is about "apartments in New York." So that is the complete subject of the sentence.

Here is the answer for the last exercise.

<u>Apartments in New York</u>　　<u>are terribly expensive</u>.
　　　　Complete Subject　　　　　　　　Predicate

In the above answer, *apartments* is called a simple subject. The total phrase (apartments in New York) is called the complete subject.

Simple Subject:　Apartments

Complete Subject:　Apartments in New York

EXERCISES

Here is a sentence similar to the one used in the last exercise

Houses in California are terribly expensive.

1. What is the complete subject of the sentence above?

_____

2. What is the simple subject of the sentence?

_____

3. What is the predicate?

_____

4. Does the predicate make a statement about the simple subject or the complete subject?

_____

If two sentences have different complete subjects but identical predicates, they can be combined into one sentence by joining the complete subjects with *and*.

EXERCISES

Combine each pair of sentences into one sentence with the conjunction *and*.

   1. Sentence A: Apartments in New York City are terribly expensive.
         Sentence B: Houses in California are terribly expensive.

_____

   2. Sentence A: The steak from Omaha is very tasty.
         Sentence B: The cornbread from your grandmother is very tasty.

_____

Here is the answer for the last exercise.

    The steak from Omaha and the cornbread from your grandmother *are* very tasty.

Note that the verb in the answer is *are* even though the verbs in the original sentences are *is*. The answer has a compound subject, so it requires a plural verb. Make sure that you use a plural verb in the next answer.

EXERCISE

Combine the sentences below into one sentence with the conjunction *and*.

Sentence A: The red cup in the sink belongs to Jim.
Sentence B: The book on the kitchen table belongs to Jim.

_____

34

USING *AND* TO COMBINE SENTENCES WITH IDENTICAL SUBJECTS BUT DIFFERENT (OR PARTLY DIFFERENT) PREDICATES

Sometimes sentences with identical subjects but different predicates can be joined with *and*. Recall that in a simple sentence such as the following one, everything after the subject is called the predicate.

<u>Larry</u>   <u>swims every day in the summer</u>.
Subject   Predicate

EXERCISES

1. Copy this sentence.

   Larry exercises in the gym during the winter.

_____

2. In the sentence you just copied, underline the subject and write *subject* under it.

3. In the same sentence you just copied, underline the predicate and write *predicate* under it.

Here are two sentences with identical subjects but different predicates.

Sentence A: Larry swims every day in the summer.

Sentence B: Larry exercises in the gym during the winter.

These sentences can be joined by *and*. The subject is written just once at the beginning. Then each of the predicates is written with *and* between them.

EXERCISE

Rewrite these sentences as one by using the conjunction *and*.

Larry swims every day during the summer.
Larry exercises in the gym during the winter.

_____

To answer the last exercise, first the subject must be written.

Larry

Then the predicate for the first sentence is written.

Larry *swims every day during the summer*

Next the conjunction *and* is added.

Larry swims every day during the summer *and*

Finally, the second predicate is written.

Larry swims every day during the summer and *exercises in the gym during the winter*.

EXERCISES

In each exercise, combine the sentences with the conjunction *and*.

1. Sentence A: Lisa plays on our college basketball team.
   Sentence B: Lisa hopes to become a professional basketball player.

_____

---

2. Sentence A: The mother bear growled at the hikers when they approached her cubs.
   Sentence B: The mother bear then led the cubs away from the people.

_____

3. Sentence A: Anita packed three thoughtful presents in a box.
   Sentence B: Anita sent the box to Alaska where her sister Carol would be spending her birthday on an assignment from the Air Force.

_____

4. Sentence A: The strawberry shortcake looks delicious.
   Sentence B: The strawberry shortcake tastes even better than it looks.

_____

5. Sentence A: My big sister who is in high school rereads all of the papers she writes several times.
   Sentence B: My big sister who is in high school revises the papers to improve them before turning them in to her teacher.

_____

Sometimes the predicates in a pair of sentences are not totally different. They may be partly the same and partly different. An example is shown in the next exercise.

EXERCISES

Compare these sentences.

Sentence A. My brother bought three chocolate sundaes.

Sentence B. My brother ate three chocolate sundaes.

1. Copy Sentence B.

_____

2. In the sentence you copied, underline all of the words that are identical to the words in Sentence A.

Here is the answer for the last exercise.

<u>My brother</u> ate <u>three chocolate sundaes</u>.

The only word that is not underlined is *ate*. Sentences A and B are identical in everything but their verbs (*bought* and *ate*). Such sentences can often be combined with *and*, as illustrated by the next exercise.

EXERCISE

Rewrite the following sentence with *bought and ate* in the blank space.

My brother _____ three chocolate sundaes.

_____

Your answer for the last exercise shows how to combine two sentences that are partly the same and partly different. Write the parts that are the same just once and join the parts that are different with *and*. Use this approach in the next exercise.

EXERCISE

Combine these sentences with the conjunction *and*.

Sentence A: Our dog chased the frisbee as it flew through the air.
Sentence B: Our dog caught the frisbee as it flew through the air.

_____

In answering the last exercise, the following three steps are involved.

1. The part at the beginning where the sentences are the same is written just once.

   Our dog

2. The parts of the sentence that are different are written out completely and joined by *and*.

   Our dog *chased and caught*

3. The part at the end where the sentences are the same is written just once.

   Our dog chased and caught *the frisbee as it flew through the air.*

In the next exercise, the sentences differ by more than just one word. But the same approach can be used to join them with *and*.

In answering the last exercise, the first step is writing the part at the beginning of the sentences where they are the same.

> When I was younger, every Saturday Mom

The next step is adding the parts where the sentences are different joined with *and*.

> When I was younger, every Saturday Mom *took me to the library* **and** *checked out about 10 books I liked*

The final step is writing the part at the end where the sentences are the same.

> When I was younger, every Saturday Mom took me to the library and checked out about 10 books I liked *to help me improve my reading skill.*

4. Sentence A: Although only ten, my little sister Tanya, who says she wants to be a veterinarian, owns more live pets than any of her cousins or classmates.
Sentence B: Although only ten, my little sister Tanya, who says she wants to be a veterinarian, owns more stuffed animals than any of her cousins or classmates.

CHAPTER

35

USING *OR* TO COMBINE SENTENCES WITH DIFFERENT SUBJECTS BUT IDENTICAL PREDICATES

In Chapter 33, you used *and* to combine sentences with different subjects but identical predicates. In this chapter, you will use *or* to combine such sentences. An example is shown in the following exercise.

EXERCISE

Combine these sentences by joining the subjects with *or* and then writing the predicate just once after these subjects.

Sentence A: Leslie will have the car fixed.
Sentence B: Jessica will have the car fixed.

The answer for the last exercise can be obtained by following two steps.

1. The subjects are joined with *or*.

Leslie or Jessica

2. The predicate is written after these two subjects.

> Leslie or Jessica *will have the car fixed.*

Here is a pair of sentences that could be combined with *and* or *or*.

> Sentence A: Jim will meet Cathy at the airport.
> Sentence B: Paul will meet Cathy at the airport.

If both men will meet Cathy, then the sentences can be combined with *and* like this.

> Jim and Paul will meet Cathy at the airport.

But if only one of the two men will meet her, then the sentences should be combined with *or*, as in the next exercise.

EXERCISE

Combine the sentences by joining the subjects with *or* and then writing the predicate just once after these subjects.

> Sentence A: Jim will meet Cathy at the airport.
> Sentence B: Paul will meet Cathy at the airport.

_____

Inexperienced writers sometimes use the wrong form of a verb in a sentence whose subject is two singular subjects joined by *or*. You will correct the type of error they make in the next exercise.

EXERCISE

Rewrite this sentence with *are* replaced by *is*.

> Mr. Norton or Mr. Walsh are responsible for your account.

_____

Here is the answer for the last exercise.

> Mr. Norton or Mr. Walsh is responsible for your account.
> ↑
> Singular Verb

When two singular subjects are joined by *or*, a singular verb is needed in the combined sentence.

This pattern is illustrated in the next exercises.

EXERCISES

1. Rewrite this sentence with *are* replaced by *is*.

   Coffee or soda are included in the price of the meal.

   _____

2. Rewrite this sentence with *are* replaced by *is*.

   A portable radio or a gold-plated pen are given to everyone who test-drives one of their new cars.

   _____

If two plural subjects are joined by *or*, the situation is different.

When two plural subjects are joined by *or*, a plural verb is needed in the combined sentence. Use this information to do the next exercise.

EXERCISE

Rewrite these sentences as one sentence by joining their subjects with *or*.

Sentence A: My relatives are constantly asking to borrow my new car.
Sentence B: My wife's relatives are constantly asking to borrow my new car.

_____

In the last exercise, both of the original sentences have plural subjects, so the combined sentence has a plural verb *are*. Here is the answer.

My relatives or my wife's relatives are constantly asking to borrow my new car.

Use the same reasoning to answer the next exercise.

EXERCISE

Combine these sentences by joining the subjects with *or*.

Sentence A: Six cars are needed to carry all of this equipment.
Sentence B: Two trucks are needed to carry all of the equipment.

_____

If a singular subject and a plural subject are joined by *or*, the verb depends on which subject is closer to the verb.

Use this principle in the next exercise.

EXERCISE

Rewrite this sentence with the correct verb.

Rice or potatoes *is/are* served with every meal.

_____

In the last exercise, the noun *potatoes* is closer to the verb, and it is plural. Therefore, the plural verb (*are*) is correct. Here is the answer.

Rice or potatoes *are* served with every meal.

In the next exercise, the same subjects are used, but their order is reversed.

EXERCISE

Rewrite this sentence with the correct verb.

Potatoes or rice *is/are* served with every meal.

_____

The following exercise involves the same type of decision.

EXERCISE

Rewrite this sentence with the correct verb.

Ruth's dog or Rita's chickens *wake/wakes* me every morning.

_____

In the last exercise, the subject includes the nouns *dog* and *chickens*. The plural noun *chickens* is closer to the verb. Therefore, the verb must be plural.

Here is the answer.

Ruth's dog or Rita's chickens *wake* me every morning.

EXERCISES

1. Rewrite the answer from the last exercise with the order of the subjects reversed and the correct verb.

   _____

2. Rewrite this sentence with the correct verb.

   Loud music or blaring televisions *prevent/prevents* me from concentrating on my homework.

   _____

3. Rewrite this sentence with the correct verb.

   Blaring televisions or loud music *prevent/prevents* me from concentrating on my homework.

   _____

USING *OR* TO COMBINE SENTENCES WITH IDENTICAL SUBJECTS BUT DIFFERENT (OR PARTLY DIFFERENT) PREDICATES

Sometimes sentences with identical subjects but somewhat different predicates can be combined with *or*.

Here are such sentences.

I will *go to the movie with you.*

I will *visit you at home after the movie.*

These sentences have the same subject *I* and helping verb *will*. But they differ after *will*. The repeated words (*I will*) can be written just once and the other words can be connected with *or*.

EXERCISE

Combine these sentences by writing their identical sections just once and joining their different sections with *or*.

    Sentence A: I will go to the movie with you.
    Sentence B: I will visit you at home after the movie.

_____

In the next exercise, the sentences are identical in their beginnings and endings. They differ in the middle sections.

EXERCISE

Combine these sentences by writing their identical section just once and joining their different sections with an *or*.

    Sentence A: We can take algebra in our freshman year.
    Sentence B: We can take home economics in our freshman year.

_____

Here is the answer for the last exercise.

    We can take algebra or home economics in our freshman year.

EXERCISE

Combine these sentences into one sentence by writing their identical sections just once and joining their different sections with *or*.

    Sentence A: Daniel wants to study forestry in college.
    Sentence B: Daniel wants to study engineering in college.

_____

Here is the answer for the last exercise.

    Daniel wants to study forestry or engineering in college.

Here are two possible answers for the last exercise.

    You can order a copper or silver bracelet.

    You can order a copper bracelet or a silver bracelet.

The second answer repeats the word *bracelet*. It illustrates that identical words can be repeated in a combined sentence if doing so makes the sentence sound better or conveys the meaning more fully. In this case, the second answer may be preferred because it emphasizes that there are two kinds of bracelets.

EXERCISE

In each exercise, combine the sentences using the conjunction *or*.

1. Sentence A: Lorna will play tennis this afternoon.
   Sentence B: Lorna will go to the track meet this afternoon.

   _____

2. Sentence A: Denise will ski in the mountains on spring break.
   Sentence B: Denise will surf at the beach on spring break.

   _____

3. Sentence A: Dad should mow the lawn on Saturday.
   Sentence B: Dad should clean the garage on Saturday.

   _____

4. Sentence A: We can travel around the country this summer.
   Sentence B. We can take a college course in computer programing this summer.

   _____

CHAPTER

37

USING *BUT* TO COMBINE SENTENCES THAT ARE PARTLY IDENTICAL AND PARTLY DIFFERENT

Sometimes sentences that are partly identical and partly different can be combined with *but*. An example is shown in the next exercise.

EXERCISE

Combine these sentences by writing their subjects just once and joining their predicates with *but*.

Sentence A: Robin sprained her ankle.
Sentence B: Robin finished the race.

These sentences have identical subjects but different predicates.

<u>Robin</u>   <u>sprained her ankle</u>.
Subject   Predicate

<u>Robin</u>   <u>finished the race</u>.
Subject   Predicate

They can be combined by writing the subject just once and joining the predicates with *but*.

> *Robin* sprained her ankle ***but*** finished the race.

The predicates are joined with *but* rather than *and* because they form a contrast. Ordinarily a runner who sprains an ankle does not finish a race. The fact that Robin did is somewhat unexpected.

A writer uses *but* to signal readers that something unexpected follows. Thus, *but* is appropriate for joining the predicates in the exercise above.

In the next exercise, the sentences are identical in more that just their subjects.

EXERCISE

Combine these sentences by writing the identical parts just once and joining the parts in which they differ with *but*.

    Sentence A: Coach O'Brien speaks kindly.
    Sentence B: Coach O'Brien speaks firmly.

The sentences in the last exercise are identical in more than just the subjects. They also have identical verbs. The sentences differ only in the adverbs (*kindly, firmly*) that follow the verb. Since these adverbs present a contrast, they can be joined with *but*.

EXERCISES

Combine the sentences in each exercise by writing their identical parts just once and joining the parts in which they differ with *but*.

    1. Sentence A: Grandma is old.
       Sentence B: Grandma is active.

    2. Sentence A: The mall opens at 10 a.m. on weekdays.
       Sentence B: The mall opens at noon on Sundays.

---

3. Sentence A: Riding skateboards is exciting.
    Sentence B: Riding skateboards is dangerous.

    _____

4. Sentence A: Rain brings spring flowers.
    Sentence B: Rain also brings spring floods.

    _____

5. Sentence A: Charles likes ice skating.
    Sentence B: Charles dislikes skiing.

    _____

6. Sentence A: Marie wanted a car for graduation.
    Sentence B: Marie received a wristwatch for graduation.

    _____

7. Sentence A: Toby loves to play football.
    Sentence B: Toby also wants to maintain a high grade point average, so he
    studies for several hours every night.

    _____

CHAPTER

USING *AND* TO COMBINE THREE SENTENCES THAT ARE PARTLY THE SAME AND PARTLY DIFFERENT

Here is how three sentences that are partly identical can be combined.

    Sentence A: Carol speaks Spanish.
    Sentence B: Carol speaks Japanese.
    Sentence C: Carol speaks Chinese.

      Combined: Carol speaks Spanish, Japanese, and Chinese.
                               ↗   ↖
                            Comma   Comma

Notice that a comma is placed between *Japanese* and *Chinese*, and that another comma is placed before *and*.

EXERCISES

1. Combine these three sentences into one sentence, using the pattern shown above in the example.

   Sentence A: Monkeys like grapes.
   Sentence B: Monkeys like bananas.
   Sentence C: Monkeys like oranges.

   _____

2. Rewrite this sentence with a comma placed after *tea*.

   The airline served coffee, tea and soda.

   _____

If you look for sentences like those above in newspapers and magazines, you find that some writers omit the comma before *and*. However, including the comma before *and* often makes a sentence easier to read. Include such commas in the exercise below.

EXERCISE

Combine these three sentences into one sentence using the pattern shown in the above exercises.

   Sentence A: To stay fit, Steve swims.
   Sentence B: To stay fit, Steve runs.
   Sentence C: To stay fit, Steve lifts weights.

In the last exercise, all three sentences begin with the same four words:

   To stay fit, Steve

In the answer, these four words are written just once. The other words are joined with commas and *and*.

   To stay fit, Steve swims, runs, and lifts weights.

In the next exercise, note that the three sentences are identical at the beginning and at the end. In combining the sentences, write identical parts just once.

EXERCISE

Sentence A: A cold front brings cold air to an area.
Sentence B: A cold front brings clouds to an area.
Sentence C: A cold front brings rain to an area.

Here is the answer for the last exercise.

A cold front brings cold air, clouds, and rain to an area.

Comma   Comma

EXERCISES

For each exercise, combine the three sentences using the pattern shown in this chapter.

1. Sentence A: For dessert my aunt offered us chocolate brownies.
    Sentence B: For dessert my aunt offered us blueberry pie.
    Sentence C: For desert my aunt offered us strawberry ice cream.

2. Sentence A: With the money I earned from my part-time job, I went to the Rose Bowl Game.
    Sentence B: With the money I earned from my part-time job, I went to the Orange Bowl Game.
    Sentence C: With the money I earned from my part-time job, I went to the Hula Bowl Game.

3. Sentence A: The pirate's chest held gold coins worth thousands of dollars.
    Sentence B: The pirate's chest held emerald rings worth thousands of dollars.
    Sentence C: The pirate's chest held ropes of pearls worth thousands of dollars.

4. Sentence A: My cousins, who range in age from six to sixteen, hunted shells at the beach.
   Sentence B: My cousins, who range in age from six to sixteen, built sand castles at the beach.
   Sentence C: My cousins, who range in age from six to sixteen, rode their surfboards at the beach.

---

5. Sentence A: The cruise ship had a swimming pool for passengers to get a little exercise.
   Sentence B: The cruise ship had a tennis court for passengers to get a little exercise.
   Sentence C. The cruise ship had an air-conditioned gymnasium for passengers to get a little exercise.

---

6. Sentence A: Mary likes to ski in the winter.
   Sentence B: Mary likes to ride her surfboard in the summer.
   Sentence C: Mary likes to play golf during the spring and fall.

CHAPTER

COMBINING SENTENCES WITH EXPRESSIONS SUCH AS *IN ADDITION TO* AND *AS WELL AS*

This chapter discusses the use of expressions such as *along with* to add information to a sentence. The following exercises begin the discussion.

EXERCISES

1. Combine these sentences with *and*.

   Sentence A: Sally is vacationing in Miami.
   Sentence B: Darlene is vacationing in Miami.

   _____

2. Rewrite the following sentence with *as well as Darlene* inserted after *Sally*. Place commas before and after the inserted words.

   Sally is vacationing in Miami.

   _____

Here is the answer for Exercise 1.

<u>Sally and Darlene</u>   <u>are</u>   vacationing in Miami.
  Compound Subject   Plural Verb

Note that the verb in the answer is *are*, which is plural. A plural verb is needed because the subject is a compound subject with the conjunction *and*.

Now let us look at the answer for Exercise 2.

Sally, as well as Darlene, *is* vacationing in Miami.

When a singular subject is followed by an expression like *as well as*, the verb in the sentence must be singular. This pattern is illustrated again in the next exercise.

EXERCISE

Rewrite this sentence with *as well as her sister* inserted after *Clara*. Place commas before and after the inserted words.

Clara sings in the church choir.

Here is the answer for the last exercise.

Clara, as well as her sister, *sings* in the church choir.
↗
Singular Verb

Note that the verb in the sentence (*sings*) ends in *s* and is therefore singular. Inserting a phrase like *as well as her sister* does not make the subject plural. It does not make the subject a compound subject. The information it provides is considered background information. The original subject (*Clara*) remains the focus of attention.

EXERCISE

Rewrite this sentence with the correct verb.

Gilbert, as well as his brother, *play/plays* in our school's jazz band.

The correct verb for the sentence in the last exercise is the singular verb *plays* because the subject remains singular.

Here is the correct answer.

Gilbert, as well as his brother, plays in our school's jazz band.

The same pattern is illustrated in the next exercise.

EXERCISE

Rewrite this sentence with *in addition to our regular TVs* inserted after *TV*.

A wrist TV is on sale this week.

_____

Here is the answer for the exercise above.

A wrist TV, in addition to our regular TVs, is on sale this week.

Of course, if the subject and verb in a sentence are plural, they remain plural when an insertion is made. Use this information for the next exercise.

EXERCISE

Rewrite this sentence with *in addition to my brother* inserted after *sisters*.

My sisters are now away at college.

_____

Here is the answer to the above exercise.

My sisters, in addition to my brother, are now away at college.

The remaining exercises provide additional illustrations of the fact that a singular verb remains singular even when an expression like *in addition to* is inserted after the subject.

EXERCISES

1. Rewrite this sentence with *as well as other expensive American cars* inserted after *Car*.

   The Lincoln Town Car puts more emphasis upon appearance and comfort than on handling and performance.

   _____

2. Rewrite this sentence with *as well as the music of the Rolling Stones and various other rock groups* inserted after *Presley*.

   The music of Elvis Presley has remained popular here for several decades, showing that *rock and roll* is a part of American culture.

   _____

3. Rewrite this sentence with *in addition to most other political leaders* inserted after *President*. Place commas before and after the inserted material.

   Our current President believes that all American students should learn American history.

   _____

4. Rewrite this sentence with *along with the governors of several other states* inserted after *state*. Surround the inserted material with commas.

   The governor of my home state is trying to figure out how to make the public educational system more effective.

   _____

5. Rewrite this sentence with *as well as her best girl friend* inserted after *sister*.

   My sister plays the saxophone and the clarinet in our school's jazz band.

   _____

Note that you are not asked to use commas in the last exercise. Some writers do not use commas with such insertions when the insertions are fairly short. Nevertheless, the verb matches the subject of the original sentence and is not affected by the insertion.